D0507712

LABOUR AND UNEMPLOYMENT
1900-1914

A

Labour and Unemployment 1900-1914

KENNETH D. BROWN

David & Charles : Newton Abbot

ISBN 0 7153 5301 2

Set in eleven point Baskerville
and printed in Great Britain
by W. J. Holman Limited Dawlish
for David & Charles (Publishers) Limited
South Devon House Newton Abbot Devon

To my parents

Contents

List of illustrations

*All the above are reproduced by permission of the
Trustees of the British Museum*

Introduction

VIEWED FROM THE somewhat unreliable standpoint of the 1930s the Edwardian age in Britain assumed for many a quality akin to that of the Garden of Eden: a sort of golden age, untarnished by the horrors of modern warfare, nationalism, financial crises, or mass unemployment. The simple passage of time and a considerable amount of research have both combined, however, to show the other side of this picture, revealing and stressing the insecurities, the tensions, and the social inequalities of Edwardian society. The period saw governments, both Liberal and Conservative, striving to cope with newly revealed social problems—bad housing, old age, undernourishment, and unemployment. The outcome of their strivings was the foundation, albeit somewhat shaky, of the modern welfare state.

It was also in the Edwardian years that the organised working classes emerged as a genuine, independent political force, and this book seeks to examine the attitudes and actions of the British labour movement in just one of the fields with which government was becoming increasingly concerned—unemployment. How far was the movement able to influence government? Was the new Labour Party as feeble as its left-wing critics have often asserted? Did the working-class groups have any realistic proposals of their own and, if so, how did they try to realise them? How did the organised working classes react to new legislation designed for their benefit? These are some of the questions that this book sets out to answer.

CHAPTER 1

The days of the Social Democrats, 1900-1904

BY THE LAST decade of the nineteenth century many Englishmen had come to accept the need for substantial state intervention in order to tackle the problems of poverty. Hitherto, the poor had been dealt with under the none-too-tender Poor Law Amendment Act of 1834 or by the numerous private charitable bodies. The former operated on the principle that state relief should be made as unpleasant as possible in order to deter all but the most desperate from applying, and it was consequently very unpopular. By the late 1860s policy had been relaxed somewhat towards those who manifestly could not help themselves, but this was accompanied by a much more stringent attitude towards those in receipt of out relief, which in practice usually meant the unemployed. The main agency of private philanthropy, the Charity Organisation Society (COS), was also much disliked, largely because of its underlying philosophy that poverty was the result of some personal defect. 'In charitable work,' wrote Helen Bosanquet, one of the society's workers, 'we devote ourselves to those who are weak, who have in some way failed.'[1] Help was given to those who were deemed deserving, but only after the most rigorous investigation of the individual's circumstances—which was again greatly resented—and with the intention of ensuring that the recipient remained self-reliant.

What really swung public opinion behind the demand for state action was the revelation that neither the poor law nor private charity was doing more than scratching the surface of the problem. Jack London, the American socialist writer who

lived for some months in London's East End in order to see
for himself what conditions were really like, claimed in 1903
that neither relief system had achieved anything 'beyond relieving an infinitesimal fraction of the misery'.[2] The failure of
the existing machinery was made abundantly obvious when
social surveys carried out in London by Charles Booth and in
York by Seebohm Rowntree suggested that over one third
of Britain's urban population was living at or below subsistence level. Such a situation caused even greater concern when
large numbers of recruits for the army had to be rejected as
unfit for service at the time of the Boer War, a lesson with
added import for those who had been watching with some
alarm the growing economic and military strength of Germany
so clearly foreshadowed in the Franco-Prussian War of 1870-1.[3]

Fear for Britain's world position was not the only force working to convince Englishmen that state action was necessary to
deal with the conditions exposed by Booth and Rowntree.
There was a great upsurge of humanitarian sentiment, well
illustrated in the attempts of William Booth to apply the social
content of the Christian gospel through his Salvation Army
movement. Some of this sentiment, however, was less genuinely
altruistic, springing from the fear that working-class poverty
might breed revolution. This is suggested very strongly by the
fact that in 1886 the Lord Mayor's Mansion House Fund,
established to relieve the unemployed, shot up from £19,000
to £72,000 in the two days immediately following demonstrations in the heart of London's clubland. The rioters, most of
them unemployed workers from the East End, were led by
members of the Social Democratic Federation (SDF) who had
been drilling them for some time under the direction of H. H.
Champion, a former soldier. It was not without significance
that shortly after these outbreaks of unrest the President of the
Local Government Board, Joseph Chamberlain, issued a circular making provision for the establishment of unemployment
relief works by local councils, the first attempt to separate the

unemployed from other poor law cases.

One other factor which also contributed to the shift of public opinion was the growing political significance of the working classes. After the Reform Acts of 1867 and 1884 most working men enjoyed the right to vote and by the Local Government Act, also of 1884, the local government franchise was extended and the property qualification for poor law guardians was abolished. All this meant that the voice of the working classes was heard and considered increasingly in the counsels of government. It was, furthermore, a voice which was becoming more articulate and more highly organised. The Trades Union Congress (TUC) had been established in 1867, the SDF in 1883, followed ten years later by a second socialist body, the Independent Labour Party (ILP), and in 1900 by the Labour Representation Committee (LRC).

In 1909 a rising young economist, W. H. Beveridge, wrote that unemployment was fundamental to the whole question of poverty. 'Workmen today,' he said, 'are men living on a quicksand, which at any moment may engulf individuals, which at uncertain intervals sinks for months or years below the sea surface altogether.'[4] Given this, and the fact that socialism came to the fore in England at a time when unemployment was exceptionally heavy, it was not surprising that socialists in particular devoted a great deal of attention to the subject. Indeed, E. R. Pease, an early Fabian representative on the LRC, later suggested that 'excessive attention' had been lavished on the unemployed by English socialists.[5] But unemployment was no respecter of persons and all sections of the organised working-class movement joined, with varying degrees of enthusiasm, in the discussions about social policy which characterised late Victorian England.

They generally agreed that the introduction of labour-saving machinery and its corollary, cheap labour, were among the leading causes of unemployment. Thus the early programme of the ILP included the abolition of child labour, and TUC conferences passed similar resolutions in 1895, 1896, and 1897, although they were usually opposed by textile workers who benefited from cheap child labour. Others felt that the answer to this aspect of unemployment lay simply in a reduction of the hours of work, often associating with this plans for the reduction of systematic overtime, as in the resolution moved by Henry Broadhurst at the TUC conference in 1886. The demand for a statutory eight-hour day was made initially by the SDF in the early 1880s, and after the publication in 1886 of Tom Mann's pamphlet, *What a compulsory eight hour day means to the workers*, it was taken up by London building trade workers and then spread to the whole labour movement. Throughout the late eighties and early nineties the eight-hour cry was raised, but there were frequent clashes at labour conferences between its advocates and those who believed that it would result in smaller wages and a gradual loss of work to foreigners. Although Keir Hardie, founder of the ILP, took the matter up in Parliament in 1894 and a Bill was introduced the following year, nothing had been achieved by the turn of the century. This was due partly to labour's weak parliamentary position and partly to the set-back the campaign received when the Amalgamated Society of Engineers was defeated after a long and costly strike for the eight-hour day in 1897. In any case, trade unionists were divided over both aims and means. Some wanted a general eight-hour day while others preferred a reduction for certain categories of workers as an initial step. They were also split over whether the change was to be secured by legislative action or by collective industrial effort, a division made manifest when the TUC organised a plebiscite on this point in 1888.[6]

Another group of suggestions which found considerable support as possible remedies for unemployment related to the land. Rural immigration into towns undoubtedly was increasing competition for unskilled jobs, depressing wages, and accelerating the descent in the social and economic scale of the older and less able urban workers. To keep agricultural labourers in the countryside, it was argued, adequate facilities should be provided, notably decent housing and security of tenure. For this purpose TUC conferences frequently called for a reform of the country's land laws, for example in 1887, 1889, and 1895. One Social Democrat claimed that the land should be nationalised and the various councils given the power to organise the urban unemployed into the agricultural proletariat of the future.[7] Some envisaged this being done in special labour colonies where the unemployed could be trained for future careers as smallholders. The leading labour advocate of such colonies was George Lansbury, although Keir Hardie and Will Crooks also supported the idea. The latter told his biographer:

> I maintain that even the town wastrel takes more kindly to the land than to anything else. Of course, I know that before he can be made any use of he must be trained, but then it is well known that I favour farm colonies for training him.[8]

A rural note was also evident in the schemes of national works which, it was felt, the government should prepare and set in operation when unemployment grew unusually high. Afforestation was one of the most popular, but harbour construction, coast and land reclamation also found a place in Ben Tillett's resolution at the 1895 meeting of the TUC. The previous year, Hardie, in raising the question in the House of Commons, had suggested that in times of severe distress the government should anticipate works scheduled for some future date, such as the construction of new warships or roads. The TUC was sufficiently interested in the idea of government finance for remunerative local works of a similar nature to organise a members' ballot about it in 1894.

If many Englishmen, workers and otherwise, could give tacit assent to most of these possible reliefs for unemployment,

B

there were few in 1900 who agreed with Hardie, Henry Hynd-man, Robert Blatchford, and other socialist leaders, that they were all mere palliatives and that the only solution was the abolition of capitalism in favour of socialism. To socialists, cheap labour, technological redundancy, and trade fluctuations were not basic causes of unemployment at all, but were rather symptoms of capitalist organisation. The programme presented by the ILP to the International Socialist Congress in July 1896 commenced with the assertion that unemployment was the inescapable outcome of capitalism and would only disappear when capitalism itself was overthrown. Only production for use, as opposed to profit, argued socialists, would lead to the eradication of unemployment, hence the frequent demands made for the nationalisation of monopolies and basic economic resources such as mines, railways, and canals.

The logical conclusion of this line of argument was that as the state was responsible for maintaining the economic system which produced unemployment, it should also be responsible for supporting the unemployed. At the ILP's 1895 conference the Huddersfield Branch moved a resolution claiming that one of the citizen's inalienable rights should be the 'right to work' and to enjoy the fruits of his own labours. A similar resolution from the Cardiff Branch stated that as a first step towards amelioration Parliament should recognise its duty to find work for all who needed it. In really bad times Exchequer grants should be made to all local authorities unable to pro-vide work for their unemployed.[9] Earlier in the same year H. Russell Smart, mover of the Huddersfield resolution at con-ference, had written an article in Hardie's paper, the *Labour Leader*, which, while based on an assumption unacceptable to most socialists, asserted that all men possessed a natural right to work, an idea which appeared in the conference resolutions and which formed the basis of much of the labour movement's unemployment agitation before 1914. Smart argued that socialist theories on unemployment were founded on the fall-acy that it was an inevitable product of capitalism. Personally, he believed that capitalism would not die until unemployment had been vanquished, a complete reversal of orthodox socialist doctrine. What was needed, he contended, was a minimum wage and shorter hours to reduce the volume of unemployment. For those still out of work and who had lived for at least six months in one locality the local authority should be legally bound to find work. These proposals he embodied in the form of a 'right to work' Bill.[10]

These then were the main lines along which organised labour felt that unemployment should be tackled, although there were naturally differences of emphasis and not all agreed with the assumptions of the socialists. But in the changing climate of opinion at the end of the nineteenth century the working-class movements readily favoured ideas based on the new premise that in some measure unemployment could be regulated by government control of the amount of work available, and by the re-training of those whose skills had been overtaken by technology. For those still out of work the labour movement wanted a relief system which would provide useful work for wages and be free of the stigma of pauperism and the condescension of the charity workers.

But in bringing the claims of the unemployed before the public the labour movement was hampered to some extent by the fact that the problem was one which fluctuated in intensity and the degree of public interest which could be raised depended very largely on the state of the labour market. Concern was high in the middle 1880s and the early nineties, but by 1897 the economy was entering a period of boom and the ILP national executive reported to the party conference that there had been a 'cessation of public interest in the unemployed problem'.[11] The report went on to exhort party members to be prepared for the inevitable turn of the tide, but the outbreak of the Boer War in 1899 reduced unemployment still further and it soon faded from the public mind in the excitement of war and its accompanying prosperity. It was not until 1902 when the war ended that the tide to which the ILP report had referred began to show signs of turning as the running down of war industry and the return of volunteers and reservists started to dislocate the labour market. Hundreds of demobilised soldiers returned to find their jobs filled and their prospects of finding another greatly restricted by the onset of depression. Early in March 1902 the Association for the Employment of Reserve and Discharged Soldiers contacted the Prime Minister, Lord Salisbury, drawing his attention to this difficulty, but while he promised to give it 'careful attention' he refused the association's request that he receive a deputation.[12] The first working-class organisation to take up the soldiers' cause was the SDF, whose leaders doubtless welcomed the opportunity to embrace a more popular cause after the execration they had suffered for their opposition to the war. In June the SDF paper, *Justice*, predicted that the troops would find 'their places filled and no work staring them in the face', and by October the federation was organising mass demonstrations of unemployed soldiers in Hyde Park.[13] Other SDF agitators were active elsewhere, for example in Bermondsey where meetings were arranged to protest against the council's decision to invite tenders for local authority work rather than give it to the unemployed.

In November the Commander-in-Chief, Field-Marshal Lord Roberts, and John Brodrick, Secretary of State for War, both signed a special public appeal asking employers to remember the soldiers when taking on new labour, but this was as far as anyone in official circles was prepared to go. Arthur Balfour, who had taken over the premiership in July, refused on several occasions to receive deputations from the SDF and the London Trades Council, and when Hardie tried in December to secure a parliamentary discussion on the situation the Prime Minister urbanely dismissed him, suggesting that he was exaggerating its gravity. Two days later the Speaker of the House of Commons refused to allow Hardie to introduce a motion calling on the government to make a grant of £100,000 to the local authorities for the purpose of relieving their unemployed. Shortly before the end of the year the President of the Local Government Board, Walter Long, also refused to meet a deputation from the London Trades Council which wished to place before him evidence of severe unemployment in the capital. Nor was the Liberal opposition any more concerned than the government. On Christmas Eve Sir Henry Campbell-Bannerman told a Scottish audience that the most pressing social problems facing the country were housing and temperance.[14]

In a sense his argument was correct, because the latest Board of Trade unemployment figures showed only 4.4 per cent of trade unionists out of work, and such agitation as had taken place had been of a very spasmodic and local nature. (See Table 1, page 190. All subsequent unemployment percentages are taken from this table.) But the situation was certainly bad in some areas, particularly in parts of London. It was this fact, the general indifference of most politicians, and the inability of Hardie and other Labour MPs such as John Burns to force the government's hand in Parliament, which prompted the Metropolitan District Council of the ILP to convene a meeting of representative public and labour figures on 15 December 1902 in order to consider what could be done for the unemployed and also to investigate the possibilities of establishing some permanent organisation to co-ordinate activity on their behalf. Those present at this conference included Hardie, who took the chair, James Ramsay MacDonald, secretary of the LRC, and several notable radicals such as Percy Alden, Edward Pickersgill, George Bernard Shaw, and R. Cunninghame Graham. The outcome was the creation of a provisional committee of thirty, somewhat unwieldy but necessary to accommodate the various interests present. Among the members of this committee was Alden, who was made secretary,

Hardie, S. G. Hobson of the Fabian Society and his colleague E. R. Pease, who was also on the executive of the LRC. Thus the establishment of the new committee did in fact link several important sources of labour and radical power which were well able to make their influence felt in different sectors of the community. Hardie could act as spokesman in Parliament; Alden was not only a Fabian but also a member of the Mansion House Committee; Pease and MacDonald could utilise the strength of the LRC; and Hobson could bring in the sophisticated propaganda machinery of the Fabian Society.[15]

Alden's election as secretary was no surprise, for although the meeting had been summoned under ILP auspices, his, in fact, had been the initiative behind it and in an article in the *Labour Leader* he proceeded to outline the aims and structure of the new National Unemployed Committee. Under the heading of permanent objectives he listed the establishment of a government department of ministerial status to deal exclusively with unemployment and to be responsible for such things as the notification of impending distress, the publication of information as to the availability of work, and the organisation of unemployed labour on road, forest, and farm colony works. Temporary expedients for which the committee was to agitate included the opening of local unemployment offices, shelters to accommodate the homeless poor, and the immediate implementation of works already scheduled by local authorities. The new central committee was to sit in London to give information to the press, and it was hoped to set up similar committees in all the great provincial cities.[16]

Early in 1903 Alden sent out invitations to local authorities, trade unions, and other interested bodies, inviting them each to appoint two delegates to a two-day national conference called to discuss ways and means of realising this programme. The delegates, 587 of them, duly assembled on 27 February at the Guildhall and sat politely through long and often contradictory opening speeches delivered by three most unlikely colleagues—Sir John Gorst, member for Cambridge University and one time Financial Secretary to the Treasury in a Conservative administration, Lady Frances Warwick, one of the SDF's more spectacular converts, and Sir Albert Rollitt, who had been MP for Islington South since 1886. Nor did things improve once the delegates got down to the business in hand. Three resolutions, claiming respectively that unemployment was the joint responsibility of national and local government, that the government should be pressed to take action, and that pressure should also be put on the local authorities, were all moved and debated in a manner described by the *Daily Mail* as 'vague and incoherent'.[17] The fourth resolution, however, moved by George Barnes, secretary of the Amalgamated Society of Engineers, was more practical, suggesting that 'a permanent National Organisation be formed in order to give effect to the decisions of the Conference, and that the Provisional Committee be re-appointed with power to add to its number'.[18]

The SDF regarded this whole enterprise with a very jaundiced eye. Possibly this was because the proceedings had been too mild, disappointing the hope that the conference would result in the unemployed being organised to make a thorough nuisance of themselves.[19] Certainly *Justice* complained that the resolutions had been either irrelevant or too theoretical. Hardie was accused of suppressing the London Trades Council delegates, most of whom were SDF members, for fear of offending the class susceptibilities of such an august gathering.[20] But the federation's apparent hostility to the formation of the National Unemployed Committee may simply have been due to the fact that it had not been consulted about its establishment. Indeed, early in 1903 the Social Democrats had organised their own committee to arrange agitation in London, chiefly in the form of street processions. These processions were not only designed to show the unemployed that the SDF had their best interests at heart, but also to overcome the apathy of the unemployed which had severely restricted the effectiveness of earlier agitation. In November 1902, for example, Harry Quelch, editor of *Justice*, had complained that it was 'idle to expect much help from the unemployed themselves', and it was now hoped to overcome this by organising street collections, the proceeds of which were to be shared out among the marchers.[21] Two brothers named Martin were put in charge

The unemployed in London. *Daily Graphic*, 17 Jan 1903

and they moved around the East End instructing local leaders in an effort to systematise the agitation. The results were impressive. Men from Poplar, Hackney, Tottenham, Shoreditch, Battersea, Lambeth, Edmonton, Mile End, and Southwark soon began to appear almost daily in the West End, sometimes as many as a thousand marching through the city together, and it was claimed that in January alone 20,000 unemployed men had passed through the hands of the SDF organisers.[22] The campaign culminated on the eve of Parliament's re-assembly in February when unemployed workers were marched in from almost every East End district to attend a protest demonstration in Trafalgar Square. *Justice* reported that 3,500 were present and several well-known labour personalities took part, including W. C. Steadman of the London County Council, James Macdonald the Social Democrat editor of the *London Trades and Labour Gazette*, and Harry Quelch.[23]

It would be unwise, of course, to take any of these figures at their face value, especially as both the *Labour Leader* and *The Times* put the attendance in Trafalgar Square at not more than 2,000.[24] But there can be little doubt that the campaign was successful in mobilising London's unemployed and in causing a great deal of inconvenience to the authorities and the general public. Throughout its duration letters appeared constantly in the press, a few couched in terms sympathetic to the unemployed, but the vast majority overwhelmingly hostile to the demonstrations. The main burden of the complaints was that the marchers blocked the streets and caused traffic hold-ups; that the police were far too tolerant; that the marchers were being encouraged to rely for help on public charity rather than on their own efforts, and that in consequence the processions were attracting large numbers of frauds and wastrels. Thus one critical letter claimed that the superintendent of the Clapham and Wandsworth casual wards had recently spotted in a march 'several hundreds' who frequently appeared before him as vagrants.[25] The managing director of the Central

Cyclone Company asserted that many of his employees regularly took time off to join the marches because they were so lucrative.[26] It was hardly surprising, therefore, that one paper could claim that the marches contained 'a small proportion of the deserving, a considerable proportion of hardened and habitual loafers and a good many more on the verge'.[27]

The campaign also disturbed other sections of the working-class movement. At least one trade union proudly boasted that none of its members were taking part because they were all too busy looking for work.[28] The Operative Bricklayers Society, badly hit by unemployment, rejected an SDF appeal for financial help, preferring to organise its own relief for its unemployed members. John Burns admitted that the marches had succeeded in waking London up to the existence of the unemployment problem, but he became so alarmed by the campaign's magnitude that he eventually asked the government to curtail it. Hardie also seems to have been concerned by the identification in the public mind of the unemployed with the militant and annoying tactics of the SDF, particularly as he was due to chair the conference of the National Unemployed Committee at the end of February. He totally disapproved, he said, of the 'way in which these agitations on behalf of the unemployed are taken advantage of to boom some particular organisation'.[29]

The government, too, was alarmed by the danger to public order posed by the unrestricted passage of unemployed East-Enders through the city's richer areas. No doubt memories of 1886 and 1887 were uppermost in the mind of Home Secretary Henry Akers-Douglas, who was giving the matter some serious thought, as he admitted in a letter to Lord Knollys, the King's secretary.

Please assure the King that these Processions have been engaging the most anxious attention of the Commissioner of Police and myself, and that we are using to the utmost the powers which we possess.

The two points in which these Processions are most objectionable are the collecting of money, and the obstruction of traffic.

On the first point our hands are tied by a decision of the High Court in 1886 of which the gist is that if a person, not as a regular mode of living, but for some object not in itself unlawful, goes from house to house and solicits subscriptions that is not within the prohibitions of begging in the Vagrancy Act... Of course if a man with a collecting box resorts to intimidation or otherwise brings himself into conflict with the law the Police can, and will stop him...

On the other point, processions are not in themselves illegal... and until the progress of a procession causes an unreasonable obstruction of traffic the Police have no right to interfere... It has been asserted that the Police are protecting the Processionists, but that is not so. The Police are there to protect the Public by regulating to the best of their ability the whole traffic of the streets... Though I would gladly stop the unpleasantness and inconvenience if I could, there is, I am advised, nothing more that I can do without exceeding my powers, and otherwise incurring great danger of exciting grave disorder.[30]

He went on, however, in a more optimistic vein, saying that the public was at last beginning to realise the futility of giving money to the marchers and that in consequence the incentive to take part in the processions was weakening. But his concern was evidently shared by some members of the government back bench, for shortly after Parliament re-assembled the member for Hanover Square in the West End, Colonel Legge, asked if the government was aware of the inconvenience caused by the processions and whether it was proposed to curtail them by increasing police powers. Akers-Douglas replied that the police had done their best to cope, but he agreed that Legge's suggestion was worthy of consideration.[31]

In fact, it was only three months before he presented a memorandum to the cabinet on the subject. He reported that police precautions had so far been successful but 'I am assured by the Commissioner of Police that the margin of safety was slight, and that the strain on the police, at the best, unduly heavy'. In London, the memorandum continued, one man in four had been occupied in marshalling the processions between 1 January and 18 February, and as the situation could easily get out of hand in another winter Akers-Douglas recommended that the Metropolitan Streets Act of 1867 should be amended in order to prevent the marchers from collecting money so freely. If this freedom were limited, he argued, the marches would probably peter out, and he concluded his memorandum by stressing that the matter was 'one of great importance' which should be tackled 'without delay'.[32] Within three weeks of this cabinet discussion a Bill was introduced, and it reached committee stage without any debate. Here it ran into trouble with some Liberals who thought that it would not be effective, but when Akers-Douglas stressed that he considered it quite adequate for his purpose they withdrew their opposition. The Bill then passed rapidly through both houses and received royal assent on 11 August.

This, of course, was too late to be of use in curbing the campaign which had provoked the measure's introduction, but, as it happened, this did not matter, for the Social Democrat agitation had already foundered on the twin rocks of finance and doctrine. The unemployed organisers had depended for their personal income on the results of appeals made in *Justice* and although it was claimed that the response had generally been good, the report presented at the annual conference in April 1903 showed that the federation's financial position was critical. Considerable inroads had been made into the Central

Election Fund in order to finance all aspects of the work, including the unemployment campaign.[33] Doctrinally the federation was split over the value of pursuing short-term palliative objectives, such as the amelioration of unemployment, a dispute which culminated in the expulsion of the 'impossibilists' at the stormy Easter conference. Although Hyndman and the old guard thus triumphed over those who believed that a palliative policy was a waste of time, their position might well have been strengthened had it been possible to point to any significant increase in membership as a result of the unemployment agitation. But as *The Times* said:

> The federation will, in the long run, gain nothing in popular esteem ... the class which will walk in the processions is traditionally ungrateful, and it seems to be generally understood that it will throw the S.D.F. overboard as soon as it may be convenient.[34]

At the end of the month in which Akers-Douglas finally secured the passage of his Bill unemployment stood at 5.0 per cent, ominously high for midsummer. By October the figure had crept up to 5.6 per cent, and early in November *Justice* appealed to all party members to spare no effort in renewing a vigorous agitation for the unemployed.[35] But the Home Secretary, alerted by his experiences of the previous winter, lost no time in utilising the legislation which he had so recently carried through Parliament, and on 7 November the Commissioner of Metropolitan Police issued regulations under the Metropolitan Streets Amendment Act to enable the police to keep a more stringent check on the activities of the marchers. No collection was to be taken in the streets except as specified in a permit, which could only be obtained from the commissioner. Applications for these permits had to be made at New Scotland Yard ten days in advance of the collection stating its date, purpose, place, and the numbers involved. They were valid only on the specified days and had to be produced on demand. No more than two collectors were to be positioned in any one spot. Tables, and boxes on poles (to reach upper-floor windows) were not to be used unless expressly permitted, and no collector was to annoy passers-by. Breach of any of these regulations was punishable under section twelve of the Metropolitan Streets Act of 1867. Quelch reacted angrily, claiming that 'the seamy side of our civilisation is to be turned in by police brutality, and Mr Akers-Douglas will declare with pride that "order reigns in London"—as in Warsaw'.[36] Certainly the regulations were sufficiently wide, and in some cases vague, to destroy the ease of financial collection which had been the SDF's chief carrot to the unemployed. Although they applied only to areas within six miles of London's centre, thus allowing the collectors still to flourish in the East End and the provincial cities, the decline of Social Democrat agitation in the capital in the winter of 1903 undoubtedly owed much to the cramping effects of this legislation.

To some extent, too, the ground was cut from under their feet by the swift response of many of the London boroughs to the worsening situation, and by the rapid growth of public concern. The London County Council had met on 28 October to discuss what could be done, and charitable appeals were soon appearing in the columns of the daily press with almost monotonous regularity. As November passed into December the monthly journals, particularly the *Toynbee Record*, began to carry numerous articles on the severity of the distress in the East End. On 3 December there came the most striking evidence so far that the city was at last taking the problem seriously. On that date the Mansion House Committee, whose functions had been in abeyance since 1895, was recalled.

This committee, established in 1886 to administer the fund set up by London's Lord Mayor for the unemployed, now resolved to organise a system of relief for a selected number of men on the lines of a plan which had recently appeared in the press. The scheme had been formulated by a number of prominent relief workers and required the selected men, all of whom were to have established homes as a pre-condition of selection, to take work in the country, their wages going to their families. This, it was argued, would avoid homes being broken up and would ensure that no shirkers applied. It had the further advantage that although it required substantial financial backing the work could readily be undertaken on existing farm colonies at Osea Island, Hadleigh, and Lingfield. But it was opposed by Percy Alden, who disliked the proposal to separate the man from his family, and he claimed that the plan's purpose could equally well be achieved by giving each local council twenty shillings per unemployed man in order to finance local relief works. His stand evidently had some effect, for when the sub-committee appointed to consider the plan reported just before Christmas, it was deemed necessary to stress that the borough councils had in fact been approached already but that only one, Poplar, had agreed to establish works of the sort advocated by Alden.[37]

It seems likely that in making his protest Alden was acting as spokesman for the National Unemployed Committee, which had re-convened on 10 October. Although its activities since the Guildhall conference had not been well publicised—one correspondent of the *Labour Leader* inquiring in September if it was still in existence—the committee had been quite busy during the summer.[38] At the October meeting a letter had been read from the Prime Minister refusing to receive a deputation and suggesting that the committee contact the Board of Trade with the resolutions which it had originally forwarded to him. It was thereupon decided to put pressure on the London County Council to call an early meeting of the borough authorities and to ask the President of the Board of Trade, the Free Church Conference, and the Prime Minister to see deputations, the latter on the subject of appointing a labour minister. This last objective was also to be pursued in Parliament by Hardie, and when the legislature re-assembled in 1904 he moved an amendment to the King's Speech regretting that no mention had been made of the need to create such a post with special responsibility for the unemployed.

During his speech Hardie openly admitted his brief for the National Unemployed Committee, confessing that labour men generally were deeply divided about the usefulness of any labour minister. Hardie's admission must have added to the worries of those ILP members who were afraid that their party was drifting rapidly into the Liberal orbit, a path indicated by the co-operation with radicals in the National Unemployed Committee and then by the generous Liberal support given to Hardie's unemployment amendments on the King's Speeches in both 1903 and 1904. Such fears account for the wide support given to one rank-and-file member, H. Wishart, when he suggested in June 1903 that the ILP should launch a national campaign for the unemployed behind the slogan of 'work for all'. Liberals, he contended, could not possibly support such an aim, cutting as it did at the very roots of the capitalism to which they all subscribed.[39] No national campaign was undertaken, however, and ILP agitation on behalf of the unemployed in the last months of 1903 was, like that of the SDF, virtually non-existent, apart from that organised through local initiative. The party's national leaders were concentrating their energies throughout the autumn on attacking Joseph Chamberlain's proposals for tariff reform and imperial preference, organising a series of meetings for this purpose in most of Britain's major cities. But this again attracted adverse comment from the party's unemployment lobby. Fred Wood, an officer in the Huddersfield Branch, appealed for the ILP to forget everything, especially the fiscal controversy, and to lead a national campaign to press the needs of the unemployed.[40] This plea was repeated in January by another member who wanted to know why the national leadership was wasting so much time over Chamberlain's programme.[41]

The answer was partly that, as a constituent section of a

labour alliance hoping to win seats in the next general election, the ILP could neither determine the issues on which an election was to be fought nor ignore a subject which so dominated public interest. But there was also the fact, as Hardie stressed in his speech in the House of Commons in February, that Chamberlain's supporters were making much of the tariff reform proposals as a solution to unemployment. In this they were undoubtedly aided by an unemployment index registering 6.3 per cent in December 1903. Thus Maltman Barry, once a member of the First International but now a Conservative supporter, argued that 'while the present amount of unemployment in this country is very great ... the increased trade which would come to us as a result of Mr Chamberlain's policy would absorb the whole of it'.[42] Leo Maxse, editor of the monthly, the *National Review*, predicted to Sidney Buxton, the Liberal MP for Poplar, that he would find tariff reform exciting 'great enthusiasm among our working classes'.[43] Chamberlain himself admitted more than once that if he failed to win over the working classes he was lost, and it seems clear that some of the ILP leaders appreciated the danger of their mentally associating full employment with a policy of tariff reform, hence their concentration on condemning Chamberlain's programme. Nor were the fears entirely unjustified. In September 1903 the following letter, written by the Chairman of the ILP's Willesden Branch, appeared in *The Times*:

> I crave a corner in your columns to enter my individual protest against the indecent manner in which the organised workers of this country are being cajoled and blustered into passing resolutions condemnatory to any fiscal change ... the so called leaders ... have been peregrinating through the country ... asking the working classes to condemn a proposal on which we have had as yet no definite pronouncement.[44]

Late in 1903 the TUC joined the battle, issuing a statement

C

which condemned as blacklegs all workers who supported Chamberlain. This apparently had little effect in deterring those who were already committed, for in the following April the Tariff Reform League summoned a meeting of trade unionists which resolved itself into the Organised Labour Branch, eventually assuming the name of the Trade Union Tariff Reform Association. Membership, it was decided, was to be confined to *bona fide* trade unionists and a twofold objective was adopted—the strengthening of trade unionism by employing protective tariffs to guard workers against unfair foreign competition, and the consolidation of the British Empire by the use of preferential tariffs. Both, it was argued, would ensure increased employment for British workers. The tariff reform press naturally played up the importance of this meeting, prominently displaying a statement issued at its conclusion in an effort to prove that working-class opinion was behind Chamberlain. The conference had been attended, this communiqué claimed, by representative leaders of 'a great many organisations in the chief industrial towns'.[45] But no attendance figures were given, which prompted a suspicious letter from a member of the Cobden Club. 'Can it be true,' the writer asked, 'as some busybody of a reporter alleges, that only about twenty five gentlemen took part?'[46] It was.

CHAPTER 2

The Unemployed Workmen's Bill, 1904-1905

IN SPITE OF the small attendance at its inaugural meeting, the Trade Union Tariff Reform Association was launched into what promised to be a very favourable economic atmosphere, as the early months of 1904 were marked by an abnormally high level of unemployment, averaging some 5.7 per cent. Just what this cold statistic meant in human terms is well illustrated in the following pathetic note left by one George Tagg who, unable to find work even after long months of searching, killed himself.

'My dear children,
    I cannot stand this much longer. If I can't get work to pay my way and keep you I must do something, for I am nearly off my head. If the worst comes, take care of little Debbie. Don't put her in the union if you can help it. You may manage to keep her between you. God help you to do so. You may get on better without me. Goodbye to you all. May we meet in Heaven.'[1]

The situation showed no sign of improving as the summer months drew on and MPs must have been surprised to find themselves listening to an unemployment debate in July. It was initiated by Will Crooks, elected on the LRC platform in 1903 as member for Woolwich. He wanted to know what instructions had been given to the various state departments responsible for coping with unemployment. Balfour replied that the whole matter was constantly under the government's surveillance, an evasion which earned him the sharp rebuke of the *Labour Leader*. It would, said the paper, be a great comfort to 'the hundreds of thousands of men at present unemployed ... all anxiety will now be removed, for they have the assurance that neither the demands of brewers, mine owners, nor landlords ever drive the claims of the unemployed from his mind'.[2] Certainly the Prime Minister's statement did little to calm labour fears. One socialist claimed that the situation in the coming winter would not bear thinking about unless there was an immediate improvement in the labour market.[3]

Nor were working men alone in expressing fears about the position. All through the summer months the unemployed percentage never fell below 5.7, and by September several London poor law unions were making arrangements to increase their casual ward accommodation. On 26 September a special conference of south London guardians was held at Lambeth and the delegates discussed at length whether the government should be asked to take some preventive measures. In provincial cities, too, a similar concern was apparent, and local authorities all over Britain were discussing what could be done to cope with what threatened to be a winter of severe unemployment. In Bradford £5,000 was set aside for the provision of relief works, while in Manchester the Lord Mayor asked the guardians to subsidise the council in setting up similar works, although he admitted that no solution was possible until the government itself stepped in.

In view of these indications that heavy unemployment was widely anticipated, it was not surprising that the delegates at the annual TUC conference in September exhibited a lively concern about the worsening situation. Although there were still those who argued that unemployment could be offset by pursuading everyone to join a trade union, such old-fashioned ideas scarcely accorded with the more radical sentiments of the majority of delegates. Two resolutions were passed, one calling for pressure to be put on MPs and public bodies in order to secure for local councils the power to acquire land and set up works for the unemployed, the other requesting that the parliamentary committee approach the government on the matter of creating a labour minister. The most comprehensive steps of all, however, were taken by the SDF. It was no longer possible to organise street collections in the centre of London, and in any case the federation still could not afford to undertake any sustained campaign of this sort. It intended to nurse its resources until after Christmas and then hold major demonstrations to coincide with the opening of Parliament. But in the meantime the executive decided to sponsor agitation to secure a special meeting of Parliament to deal with the unemployment situation. Local branches were urged to summon public meetings and submit resolutions to the effect that 'the question should be taken up at once and dealt with on a national basis … the government to summon at once a special Autumn Session of Parliament for the purpose of promoting legislation on behalf of the unemployed'.[4] SDF members on local councils were asked to bring this resolution up for discussion, and circulars were sent to the metropolitan guardians soliciting their support. To provide statistical backing for their case, individual branches were invited to carry out a street-by-street census of the unemployed in the main industrial centres.

Five days after the SDF announced this campaign, the government at last showed signs of responding to the growing pressures and widely expressed fears. On 6 October Walter Long announced that he had received so many representations about the state of the labour market that he had decided to call a conference of all London guardians for 14 October. He claimed that he personally was not worried, but admitted the existence of 'considerable apprehension'.[5] The Social Democrat executive immediately interpreted this as an attempt to draw attention away from the demand for an autumn sitting, and in order to prevent this happening drafted a letter which was forwarded not only to Long himself but also to all the London boards of guardians. It contained a list of proposals for tackling unemployment which included the establishment of labour colonies, an eight-hour day, and the undertaking of harbour and forestry work. It further pointed out that the problem was a national one and as such required treatment and financing on a national scale. All the recipients were asked to press for a special session in order to facilitate the passage of the necessary legislation. This was supported by *Justice* which stressed the point by carrying a large headline, something it

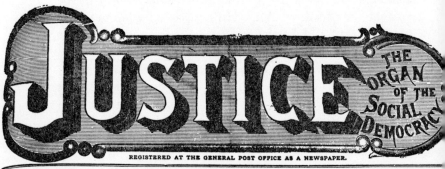

REGISTERED AT THE GENERAL POST OFFICE AS A NEWSPAPER.

No. 1,083, Vol. XXI.]   LONDON, SATURDAY, OCTOBER 15, 1904.   [WEEKLY, PRICE ONE PENNY

Published by the Twentieth Century Press, Ltd., 37a, Clerkenwell Green, London, E.C.   Subscription—Single copy 1½d., 3 months 1s. 8d., 6 months 3s. 3d., 12 months 6s. 6d., post free.
Entered at the New York Post Office as Second-class Matter.

WE DEMAND AN AUTUMN SESSION OF PARLIAMENT TO DEAL WITH THE UNEMPLOYED !

Justice, 15 Oct 1904

did not normally have. But the guardians of London did not respond very favourably. Only those in Hackney, Shoreditch, Camberwell, Poplar, and Wandsworth passed the Social Democrat resolution, while the Lambeth Board agreed to forward it to its delegates at Long's conference. When George Lansbury tried to secure its passage at the conference itself he was heavily defeated, probably because most of those attending were satisfied by Long's promise of action.[6]

It was noticeable that in opening the conference proceedings Long went to some trouble to assure his audience that he

did not share the view, current in some circles, that the country was facing an imminent and grave economic crisis. He
simply wanted, he continued, to lay the foundations of a
scheme for dealing with unemployment in a more systematic
way than ever before. Dealing first with suggestions already
put to him, he rejected outright the idea that the government
should provide a large sum of money to finance national
works, and when Lansbury moved the SDF resolution he successfully opposed it on the grounds that a special meeting of
Parliament would not achieve anything. For immediate consideration he proposed that farm colony districts be set up for
London and that in each district a local committee should be
formed, representing guardians, councils, churches, and charity groups, to sort out those who should be given work in the
farm colonies from those to be dealt with under the existing
poor law provisions. Over these committees was to be a central
body, similar to the Mansion House Committee and elected
by the local bodies. The Local Government Board, said Long,
would assist the work of all these committees by sanctioning
such administrative expenses as were necessary and paying
them out of the common poor fund. Borough councils could
also make contributions to the central fund from their rates if
they wished, and if these were considered to be *ultra vires* they
could be similarly sanctioned, under the provisions of an Act
of 1867.

On the whole these proposals were well received by the
majority of delegates and by the press, although the COS,
which was still clinging obstinately to its outmoded tenets,
accused Long of capitulating to socialist agitation and complained that the creation of public work by a public authority
was 'a most impolitic step'.[7] But in spite of these allegations,
the socialists themselves showed little enthusiasm. Hardie was
almost alone in welcoming the scheme, referring to it in
January 1905 as 'a helpful and hopeful development'.[8] *Justice*,
on the other hand, said that the conference had been nothing

more than a hollow farce designed to draw attention away from the SDF demand for an autumn session by providing a semblance of action from the central authorities. Everyone was exhorted to keep up the pressure by deputation, resolution, memorial and leaflet. All other work, it pronounced, must be laid aside.[9]

Labour's criticism of Long's plans fell roughly into three main groups. Firstly, there were those who felt that the whole concept of tackling unemployment by means of a committee system was wrong. Blatchford, for example, claimed that its operation would be much too slow.[10] Quelch objected to a committee structure because in his view its composition would be mainly bourgeois.[11] Secondly, many were undoubtedly disappointed that the burden of supporting London's farm colonies was not to be shared between all the capital's boroughs, irrespective of whether they had an unemployment problem or not. This point was made very strongly by Crooks in a letter written to Balfour in December. 'All poor parts,' he complained, 'where work-people are aggregated, have to bear abnormal burdens which should be shared, if not by the nation, then at least by the metropolis.'[12] Closely allied with this particular criticism was the fact that West Ham, one of the worst-affected areas, was excluded from the new structure because it was not a London borough. SDF speakers made much of this at a London Trades Council demonstration held in Trafalgar Square shortly before Christmas. Finally, and probably most deeply felt, came the criticisms of the financial arrangements. It was claimed by some Social Democrats that the whole scheme would fail because the local authorities would refuse to levy any rate.[13] But when working-class representatives tried to oppose a resolution put up at the first meeting of the Central (Unemployed) Body that the necessary monies be raised from voluntary subscriptions rather than from the rates, they were easily outvoted. This voluntary principle annoyed the socialists so much that Hyndman had the effrontery to claim at a public meeting chaired by the Lord Mayor of London, who was the fund's treasurer, that Long's plan was like that of General Trochu at the siege of Paris—it was not designed to work.[14]

If Long had hoped to allay the unrest and relieve the pressure of the unemployed by his plans for London, his hopes were ill-founded. Indeed, as the situation continued to deteriorate the labour organisations began to increase their agitation. At a meeting of the ILP executive, held at the end of October, it was decided to undertake a series of educational public meetings on unemployment, holding them in several important industrial cities. One party member informed the *Labour Leader* that Hardie was thinking of introducing an unemployment Bill in the forthcoming parliamentary session, and possibly this was a further step in the ILP's campaign.[15] But there is no other evidence to support the claim—for example, in the *Minutes* of the party's National Administrative Council —and while it is possible that Hardie may have been intending to introduce such a Bill on behalf of the National Unemployed Committee, it seems unlikely, as this organisation seems to have disappeared by the middle of 1904. At least, no more is heard about it. The SDF, too, was maintaining its pressure for an autumn sitting, and immediately after Long's conference sent a telegram to Balfour congratulating the government on at last ending its long months of inaction. It went on to ask about the possibility of a special session, arguing that some of the ideas which Long had mentioned required legislative orders.[16] This was supplemented by yet another appeal to the branches, this time asking them to contact their local MPs and also the government seeking their views on the matter. But only three branches are recorded as having written to the Prime Minister, and only nine MPs replied to SDF representations.[17]

The government apparently remained passive in the face of this pressure, even when the rest of the labour movement joined with the Social Democrats in demanding immediate parliamentary action. The ILP executive added its voice to the growing chorus by sending a memorandum to Balfour early in November, while Hardie raised a petition signed by fourteen MPs in favour of such a step. This had the support of the TUC, which also contacted Balfour informing him that:

> This meeting of the Parliamentary Committee of the Trades Union Congress, representing 1,500,000 workers, learns with pleasure that an appeal has been made by a number of Labour and other members of Parliament and Local Authorities urging the Prime Minister to call a special short Session of Parliament for the purpose of dealing with the unemployed question, and joins with them in pressing the matter on the Prime Minister's favourable attention.[18]

Balfour replied to all these requests in a similar vein, telling Hardie that 'if I thought that an Autumn Session of Parliament would contribute . . . I should be prepared to accept the suggestion'.[19] In a letter to Crooks he gave his reasons for refusing, stating that he felt it necessary to await the outcome of the new machinery which Long had set up, and adding that it would be unwise to place too much hope on the results of a parliamentary debate.[20]

The TUC responded to Balfour's rejection of its appeal by asking him to make arrangements for a parliamentary discussion at the beginning of the next session. It also asked the Prime Minister to receive a deputation, and in order that it should be able to present him with some concrete proposals a joint labour conference on unemployment was planned for the early new year under LRC auspices. Balfour prevaricated about this request for a deputation, but eventually admitted to his personal secretary, J. S. Sandars, that he could 'see a certain difficulty in refusing' and decided that to see it in the first weeks of February would give him an opportunity to say things which he intended anyway to say in the King's Speech.[21] Early in January 1905 Sam Woods, the TUC secretary, was summoned to Downing Street. In the event he was ill and W. C. Steadman went instead, returning with a promise from the Prime Minister that he would receive a deputation on 7 February.

Once the TUC, the ILP, and the LRC began to interest themselves seriously in the unemployment problem it was almost inevitable that the voice of the much smaller SDF would be drowned. But this should not be allowed to obscure the fact that the campaign for a special parliamentary session at the end of 1904 was started by the Social Democrats. Not without reason the executive complained at the 1905 conference that the federation had 'received little recognition for its initiative in this direction'.[22] It must have been equally galling for Social Democrats when MacDonald issued a press statement about the forthcoming LRC unemployment conference saying that it would lay down the party's official policy and that for the first time 'proposals would be pushed to the front by a permanent and active political organisation'.[23]

The Social Democrats were similarly elbowed out of the spotlight once the government decided to bring in legislation, thereby transferring the focus of attention to Parliament where both the TUC and ILP were represented. The SDF, of course, had no MPs. Long's decision to tackle the problem by Act of Parliament was hardly surprising in view of the continued rise in the unemployment rate—it reached 7 per cent at the end of November 1904—and the widespread fears that violence would soon erupt. The portents were certainly ominous. In appealing for the continuation of agitation *Justice* had claimed that 'there is better prospect than ever before of waking up the authorities to a sense of their responsibility in regard to the unemployed . . . it is our duty to see to it that we bring the requisite pressure to bear upon them'.[24] Thus in many cities Social Democrat agitators successfully channelled spontaneous unrest into effective protest. In Liverpool the complacency of the city council, which had declared that work was plentiful, was rudely shattered by a noisy mass parade of unemployed workers through the city centre, while the main Bradford workhouse was besieged early in November by 2,000 unemployed demanding work. In Manchester SDF members took over a series of meetings originally arranged by a local unemployed confectioner and turned them into mass demonstrations which so alarmed the guardians that they agreed to provide immediate relief. In the south, Brighton's most fashionable church was invaded by a large number of unemployed, again led by local Social Democrats. Fears of violence were clearly increased by London's first major demonstration of the winter, held in Trafalgar Square under the auspices of the London Trades Council, but dominated by speakers from the SDF. The *Graphic* observed that many of them had been 'very violent in tone', while the *Mail* thought that the speeches had been an open incitement to crime.[25]

On 24 January 1905, after more than a year of prevarication, the cabinet at last discussed positive legislative proposals for dealing with unemployment, basing the discussion on a paper prepared by Long. Later, when giving evidence to the royal commission on the poor laws, Long acknowledged the influence of the pressures for action which the SDF had helped to generate.

> It is all forgotten now, but during the eighteen months that the pressure of the unemployed was growing, the methods adopted by the unemployed towards all the authorities were violent in the extreme. There were crowds besieging the offices of the relieving officers . . . the boards of guardians could hardly sit in some places without safeguarding their doors. . .[26]

He went on to admit that his plan had been 'somewhat hurriedly conceived' and said that one of the considerations governing his decision to bring in a Bill had been the fact that many local authorities were constantly calling his attention to the plight of the unemployed and their agitation.[27] In this context it is worth noting that, according to *Justice*, 45 poor law unions, 12 county councils, 40 urban councils, and 3 rural district councils had passed and forwarded to the Local Government Board the SDF resolution demanding a special session of Parliament.[28] 'One of the most active agents in bringing both direct and indirect pressure to bear upon the government,' said Sir Arthur Clay, a leading figure in the COS, 'is the Social Democratic Federation.' [29]

The government was not alone in being compelled to take unemployment seriously. The Liberals, too, frequently twitted in the labour press for supporting a free trade policy that could produce such heavy unemployment and suffering, were also beginning to take an interest. The inspiration behind this was the Liberal whip, Herbert Gladstone, who had written to Campbell-Bannerman in November 1904, suggesting the establishment of one or two unofficial Liberal committees to investigate various aspects of policy, including unemployment.[30] By December these committees had come into being and a memorandum on unemployment, written by Gladstone, was circulating among the Liberal leaders. No copy survives, but its importance may be gauged from the fact that it was seen by most of the prominent men in the party—Campbell-Bannerman, Asquith, Bryce, Spencer, Tweedmouth, Fowler, Morley, and Sinclair. Gladstone took the opportunity of explaining some of his ideas in a speech at Leeds in December, advocating that the government should take a survey of all necessary national works and then use the unemployed to carry them out. This was far too radical for Sinclair and also for Bryce, who thought that the whole matter should be treated with great caution 'lest we should seem to admit that it is the duty of the State to provide work—a doctrine which would cause general alarm'.[31]

Two weeks after the cabinet's first discussion on unemployment policy, the labour deputation waited on Balfour at Downing Street. The ideas which it put to him were substantially those agreed to at the joint labour conference which had been held at the end of January, but the Prime Minister remained unimpressed. He argued against the nationalisation of industry on grounds of principle, opposed schemes of afforestation because of their cost, and rejected proposals to set the unemployed to work on coast and marshland reclamation, claiming that these were merely palliatives and did nothing to solve the basic problem. Nor did he see how the government could effectively control the flow of work in its own establishments. In a sense he could afford to be so negative because his government had at last got some positive ideas of its own, ideas which were mentioned in the King's Speech to the newly assembled parliament on 14 February 1905.

But the announcement that machinery would be set up to deal with the unemployed generally evoked little more than passing comment. Most of the daily papers selected the proposed Aliens Bill or the Redistribution Bill as the most important items of domestic legislation. The Liberal *Daily News* only referred to the Unemployment Bill in order to dismiss it as a piece of bluff that would fool no one.[32] Most labour representatives, however, were cautious, but pleased. Hardie welcomed the announcement as 'the first break in the policy of do nothingness'.[33] Arthur Henderson, who had won Barnard Castle for the LRC in 1903, thought it 'most gratifying that at last the question of unemployment finds a place in the King's Speech'.[34] The ILP decided that for the time being it would issue no more of Hardie's unemployment pamphlets, while the immediate reaction of the LRC was to call a meeting in order to prepare a statement on the Bill's proposals. Only the SDF decided to continue its agitation, arguing that the announcement was a tribute to its efforts and that they must be maintained to prevent the government from weakening. Thus a second public demonstration was fixed for 25 February, a major one already having been held to coincide with the state opening of Parliament. The editor of the *Railway Review*, the paper produced by the Amalgamated Society of Railway Servants, shared the Social Democrats' suspicions, suggesting that the proposed Bill was nothing more than an election gambit, but such accusations were unfounded.[35] It is true that Sandars had written to Balfour about the contents of the King's Speech, saying that it 'ought to be made as attractive as possible for Party reasons' as 'it may be our goodbye', but this does not indicate that the government had no intention of honouring its commitments.[36] Indeed, the Bill was discussed again by the cabinet only three days after the King's Speech was delivered to the Commons.

The memorandum which Long presented for his colleagues' consideration on this occasion dealt at length with a controversial proposal to raise money for the new scheme from the rates. He pointed out that it was generally accepted as necessary to establish some means of meeting unemployment distress before it actually occurred. As he proposed to set up bodies for this purpose, he argued, he could hardly leave them dependent on voluntary finance. One of his main purposes in introducing the Bill, he continued, was to offset the growing demand for state action to solve the problem, a demand that was popular with certain sections of the opposition and with socialists. It was quite probable that his own scheme would fail if it was denied rate aid. In this case, he concluded, the demand for direct state intervention would probably become overwhelming.[37] But this proposal to utilise the rates caused a lot of heart-searching among Conservatives, and the opposition was led by Lord Salisbury who prepared a counter-memorandum, discussed on 2 March.

This paper argued strongly against rate aid because 'it involves principles so novel that they ought only to be adopted upon the most conclusive evidence'.[38] His main fear was that once the principle had been conceded for emergencies there would be nothing to prevent future governments greatly increasing the rate contribution and turning it into a routine practice, thus encouraging the working classes to depend on the community for help rather than on their own efforts. Nor, he felt, was there any adequate safeguard against malingerers, and if rate aid was supplied voluntary aid would dry up. Anyway, he concluded, the present crisis was nearly over and the need for emergency legislation rapidly disappearing.[39] The outcome of this cabinet meeting was apparently a modified Bill, for Salisbury told Balfour a few days later that 'though the new Unemployed Bill is an improvement upon the first, I do not approve of it. I think there should be no direct access to the rates . . . for the purpose of providing work for the unemployed.' [40] He did not object, he added, to rate money being used simply to provide the machinery or to finance emigration, but he re-affirmed his hostility to Long's idea of paying the unemployed with rate monies.

Although Salisbury ended his letter to Balfour by saying that he would not press his views if there was a majority against him in the cabinet, he was not alone in his opposition to the rate aid clauses in Long's Bill, for there were powerful vested interests outside the cabinet that were equally alarmed. One of these was the COS which saw the plan as a further concession to socialist pressure. The society's secretary, C. S. Loch, argued that in practice, if not in so many words, it was admitting the existence of a right to work. He was concerned, too, that voluntary effort would die out if the rates were used, and he also thought it undesirable that by sidestepping the poor law in this way applicants for relief should avoid the penalty of disfranchisement.[41] The idea of rate aid was also opposed by the wealthy London boroughs, which resented the prospect of being rated in order to subsidise operations on behalf of the unemployed concentrated in the poorer areas. Sidney Buxton aptly summed up Long's problem when he told Campbell-Bannerman that 'his chief difficulty is with his own friends, and the richer Metropolitan Boroughs, who do not want to be rated'.[42]

For some weeks after the King's Speech the Labour representatives in the House of Commons waited patiently for the introduction of the promised legislation, ignoring the taunts of the SDF that in not raising the matter they were forgetting the interests of the class to which they belonged and which they were supposed to represent. Early in March, Long was transferred to the Irish Office and replaced at the Local Government Board by the Prime Minister's brother Gerald, but there was still no sign of the Bill, and the SDF responded to the change by circulating yet another letter, asking all local authorities to put pressure on the new minister. On 30 March the patience of the Labour MPs finally ran out and questions were thrown at Arthur Balfour with such vigour that the Speaker twice had to call for order. Three days later Balfour was wriggling even more furiously. Hardie asked if it was the government's intention to introduce the Bill before Easter under the ten minute rule as Balfour had previously hinted, and the Prime Minister replied that if this course was 'one that meets with general approval, I shall be happy to accept it'. But when Hardie pressed him to name a day, Balfour was forced to contradict himself, answering that he could not, 'nor can I venture to say that so important a Bill ought to be introduced under the ten minute rule'.[43] Discretion, however, evidently got the better of the Prime Minister's valour, and on 12 April he informed Hardie that the Bill would be brought in under the ten minute rule after all, along with the Aliens Bill.

It is tempting to interpret Long's removal to the Irish Office as a Balfourian ploy to remove him from a post in which his very genuine desire to help the unemployed had caused dissension within the party and the cabinet. But the main consideration behind Balfour's choice was simply the need to find

D

an experienced Tory squire—a class that Long typified—to satisfy the demands of the Ulster Unionists for a suitable replacement for George Wyndham. In any case, the Bill which Gerald Balfour introduced on 18 April still contained the controversial clause permitting the payment from the rates of men employed on farm colonies established under the scheme. 'It would be impossible,' he said, 'to set up statutory bodies, permanent bodies for statutory duties, and leave them entirely dependent upon voluntary subscriptions for their maintenance.' [44] The plan which he went on to outline involved the creation of local London borough distress committees, the equivalents of the existing joint committees, supervised by a central body which was to be responsible for the creation of labour registries and bureaux. The local committees were not, he emphasised, empowered to provide work—this was the task of the central body. Each borough was to make a financial contribution to the scheme equivalent to a rate of one halfpenny in the pound, to be increased to one penny at the discretion of the Local Government Board. By the time Balfour had finished describing the proposals for London his ten minutes was nearly up and he was unable to say much about the scheme outside London, except that it was to have a more optional basis.

This final statement was one that attracted a considerable amount of adverse criticism from the labour ranks. In an interview with the *Labour Leader* Hardie said that it was a major drawback and made the scheme outside the capital 'very weak and ineffective'.[45] The *Railway Review's* commentator on parliamentary affairs thought that it would lead to a flood of provincial unemployed descending on London in the mistaken belief that work would automatically be found for them there.[46] Immediately after the Bill's first reading, the parliamentary committee of the TUC met and passed resolutions to the effect that no plan would be deemed satisfactory that was not nationally applicable and compulsory. A second general criticism was levelled against the clause which dealt with the wages to be paid to men employed under the scheme's provisions. It was laid down that they had to be less than the amount earned in a week by a general labourer of the lowest class. The general labour unions naturally objected strongly to this, Tillett claiming at the dockers' congress that the Bill was tantamount to a state system of blacklegging.[47] The TUC, mindful of the interests of its unskilled members, also passed a resolution saying that the Bill would be unacceptable if it resulted in the unemployed being used to lower the wages of general and unskilled men. Others attacked the clause which stated that no one could apply to the distress committees for more than two years in succession, while Social Democrats claimed that even a penny rate was insufficient. Fred Knee, a prominent London member of the SDF, challenged the necessity of creating new authorities to deal with the unemployed, arguing that the existing ones could just as easily be used.[48] Quelch thought the distress committees should provide work as well as passing on applicants to the central committee.[49]

But it would be wrong to think that the organised labour movement had nothing but criticism for the Bill. Harry Quelch admitted that it did have a two-fold significance. It recognised state responsibility for the unemployed, and proposed to unify London for rating purposes.[50] His party colleague, James Macdonald, thought that the compulsory nature of the London scheme and the use of public funds were both highly acceptable features.[51] Nearly all sections, whatever else they may have thought of the Bill, interpreted it as the recognition of the state's responsibility for the unemployed. This was the view taken by speakers at both socialist party conferences in 1905, and the *Labour Leader*, while suggesting that the Bill was too timid, welcomed it because 'it establishes the principle that the State is responsible for these crises which drive so many men out of work'.[52] Such claims must have worried the government, for both the Balfours had emphasised that this was not the Bill's intention. When he later gave evidence to the commission on the poor law Gerald again stressed, as he had done in his cabinet paper, that the rate aid provision had been included precisely to avoid giving any such impression.[53] This widespread and contrary interpretation must help to explain the government's subsequent reluctance to persevere with the Bill, although at Canterbury in October Akers-Douglas went to great lengths to show that the slowness of government business during the spring had been due to the time-consuming activities of the opposition before Easter.[54]

By mid-May, however, doubts as to the government's good faith were beginning to manifest themselves, stimulated by the Prime Minister's refusal—or inability—on 19 April and again on 8 May to name a day for the measure's second reading. Unemployment still stood at over 5 per cent and in Leicester 500 unemployed men signed up to join a march on London in emulation of a group of striking boot-makers from Raunds in Northamptonshire, who had won considerable public sympathy by just such an action. Soon similar marches were being organised in other towns, much to the alarm of some of the Labour MPs, such as Crooks.[55] Ramsay MacDonald was also dismayed, feeling that 'these disorganised bodies of unemployed . . . would seriously damage the chances of securing a rational and sympathetic consideration of the Unemployed Problem'.[56] Carefully organised marches, however, were a different proposition, and, after consultation with MacDonald, Hardie set about arranging these under ILP auspices. A circular was sent to all local branches emphasising the need to keep out all rogues when recruiting men for the marches, and it stressed, too, the importance of enrolling as many as possible of the artisan class in order to make the maximum public impact. Each man, it added, was to take his own blanket and food.[57] On 18 May Hardie was able to inform the Prime Minister that marches had been arranged to start from Leeds, Manchester, Newcastle, Liverpool, Glasgow and Birmingham.

The press was full of alarmist rumours, the *Telegraph* claiming that if the Leicester idea was taken up on a wide scale, arms would be needed to quell the marchers.[58] 'The metropolis,' warned the *Express*, 'is by no means prepared to wake up and find itself the Mecca of unemployed pilgrims.'[59] On 15 May a stroke of fortune had enabled Hardie to supplement his campaign to put pressure on the government to pass the Unemployed Workmen's Bill. He explained in a circular to the branches marked 'strictly confidential':

> This is to explain what has been appearing in the Press, about Great Demonstrations in connection with the Unemployed. The whole thing has arisen out of some recent consultations with MacDonald as to how best to increase the prestige and standing of our movement . . . and to turn to most account the threatened march of Leicester's unemployed.

He went on to say that the previous day Joseph Fels, the millionaire American disciple of the land reformer, Henry George, had turned up at ILP headquarters with the offer of £200 to back some big effort on behalf of the unemployed, and that he and MacDonald had decided to undertake massive public meetings all over the country, with a major demonstration in London as the culmination of the provincial marches. For tactical reasons they had decided to ask the LRC to arrange the London meeting. 'By this means, we hope to make the gathering a huge success, whilst we get the credit.'[60] The same day, Hardie wrote to Henderson, explaining his plans and asserting that 'I am determined not to allow the bill to go under without making a big effort to save it'.[61] He added that the ILP would provide expenses of up to £150. This offer, in fact, presented some difficulties, for there was some suspicion among trade unionists about the ILP's motives, perhaps justifiably in view of Hardie's circular, but MacDonald suggested that if there was any feeling about the ILP finding all the money they should simply organise a general appeal to which the ILP could subscribe its donation.

But five days after writing to Henderson, Hardie informed his colleagues in the ILP that he had abandoned his plan for marches of the provincial unemployed on London, and it was widely claimed in the labour press that this was done because the Leicester unemployed, refusing to wait, had marched independently and spoilt the total effect. This, however, must have been an attempt to cover up more fundamental reasons, for the Leicester march did not begin until 4 June. Possibly when Hardie made his rather naive attempt to frighten the Prime Minister by telling him that several marches were already fixed, Balfour's firm reply had impressed him. 'I am of opinion that the arrangements of this house in regard to its own business ought not to be modified in one way or the other by any external demonstrations.' [62] Perhaps equally significant was the fact that this statement won the grateful support of the press, for Hardie had sometimes shown himself to be sensitive to public opinion. In any case, as the *Labour Leader* pointed out, the scheme was beginning to run into some practical difficulties.[63] Finally, and perhaps most decisive of all, there was the opposition of several of the Labour MPs. Burns noted in his diary for 24 May that his opposition to the Bill and the attempts to push it through had provoked criticism at a joint labour meeting from Henderson and Crooks, but 'we beat them in their attempt to rush us into the L.R.C. fold. Carried our point well. The rest of the men stood like rocks beside me.' [64]

But even though Hardie had given up the idea of mass marches on London he was still set on saving the Bill, especially when Gerald Balfour told a joint labour deputation on 25 May that only the total weekly wage paid to men given work under the Bill had to be less than that earned, on the average, by ordinary unskilled labourers in normal jobs. The actual hourly rate of pay could be the same, thus meeting the fears about the Bill being used to undercut union wage rates. In an article in the *Labour Leader* Hardie claimed that even with all its faults the measure was worth having because it recognised three vital principles—communal responsibility to find work, public acceptance of the expenses, and the removal of disfranchisement. Once the machinery was in existence, he argued, it would only need a trade crisis for all the restrictions to be swept away.[65] Thus despite the continued opposition of Burns and some difficulty in arranging suitable dates to avoid the holiday season, the plans for the London and provincial demonstrations went ahead. The first meeting took place at Sowerby in Yorkshire on 17 June, and three days later Gerald Balfour opened the debate on the second reading of the Un-employed Workmen's Bill. That the government had been disturbed by the labour interpretation of the measure as im-plying state responsibility was evident from the speeches of both Balfour and his predecessor, Long. The President of the Local Government Board emphasised again that there was absolutely no question of the state being obliged to find work for its unemployed, while Long accused the Bill's supporters of associating with it ideas which went much further than the government itself was prepared to go. Although the Bill was read a second time it came in for heavy criticism from the government's own back-benchers, especially Sir George Bart-ley, and from the press, the *Graphic* hopefully predicting that 'the government will recognise the dangers that lurk in this hastily drafted measure and will prudently allow it to drop'.[66]

By the end of June similar rumours were widespread in the labour press, though with varying degrees of optimism. The *Railway Review*, for example, expected that it would reach committee before disappearing.[67] The journal of the Electrical Trades Union on the other hand, expected it to be abandoned almost immediately.[68] At the beginning of July, Harry Quelch suggested that Balfour was deliberately leaving the Bill so that there would be no time to amend it, without which it would be useless.[69] There can be little doubt that this flood of rumours, and a continuing high level of unemployment, help to explain the success of the LRC's programme of demonstrations which continued throughout June, July and August, staggered in this way to allow each to be addressed by a national figure. They were organised on a scale far wider than anything which the SDF, for example, had previously achieved, and some impressively high attendances were claimed, though the accuracy of the estimates is open to question. Meetings were held in almost every major city, as the following list illustrates. Attendances, where given, are in brackets.[70]

Altrincham	Hull (3-4,000)	Portsmouth
Barrow	Hyde	(5,000)
Birmingham	Ilkeston	Pudsey (1,000)
(8-12,000)	Islington	Rochdale
Bradford	Jarrow	Rotherham
Brechin	Kilmarnock	St Helens
Bristol	Leeds	Scarborough
Burnley (2,000)	Liverpool	Sheffield
Burton	(13-14,000)	Stockport
Cardiff (1,000)	Long Eaton	Stockton
Crewe	Loughborough	Sunderland
Derby (2-3,000)	Manchester	Swansea
Dewsbury	Merthyr (2,000)	Wakefield
Dundee	Mexborough	Walthamstow
Ealing	Middlesbrough	Warrington
Eccles	Newcastle	Watford
Felling	Newport (2,000)	West Bromwich
Finsbury	Normanton	(15,000)
Gloucester	Norwich	Willesden
Grimsby	Nottingham	Wishaw
Halifax	Oldham	Woolwich
Hanley	Oxford (500)	Yeadon
Huddersfield	Plymouth (1,000)	York (1,000)

Each meeting passed a resolution welcoming the Bill as an acceptance of public responsibility to find jobs for the out-of-work, but demanding that it apply to the whole country equally, that all wage limits be removed, and that the bulk of the cost be borne by the national exchequer. Almost all the leading personalities of the labour world took part, with the notable exception of Burns. The whole campaign really reached its climax with the London meeting held on 9 July, but although some 250 trade unions and 2,000 unemployed took part the total effect was ruined by torrential rain. Nevertheless, it must have been extremely aggravating that such a successful series of demonstrations costing over £150 passed almost unnoticed. 'No conspiracy of silence, no boycott of popular agitation,' complained the *Labour Leader*, 'was ever more complete than that of last Saturday's and Sunday's Unemployed Bill demonstrations by the London Press . . . not a single reference was made to the huge meetings held in scores of towns.'[71] Nor was the London demonstration any more successful in earning public notice, the *Express* almost laconically observing the day afterwards that suicide as a means of escape from unemployment seemed to be on the increase, an observation of peculiar poignancy for the few relatives of the sixty-nine-year-old unemployed woman whose useless and unwanted body had just been removed from the River Medway.[72]

Some did claim, however, that one result of the demonstrations was a softening in the Prime Minister's attitude. There may well have been an element of truth in this, for on 13 July, just after the London meeting, Balfour announced that the Bill could go through. But he made its passage conditional on the removal of the rate aid clause and it is clear that a great deal of pressure was being exerted on the government behind the scenes, not only by its own supporters, but also by outside interests. Only a week previously the West End London boroughs had made a strong protest against the financial arrangements, and it is significant that on 17 July Balfour told a deputation of the wives of London's unemployed that a revised Bill would be drawn up once current negotiations were complete: this on the same day that a Conservative paper advised the government to relegate the measure 'to the limbo from which it should never have emerged'.[73]

The discussions about the Bill's future were evidently well advanced, as less than a week passed before Gerald Balfour presented the revised version to the House of Commons. It was now envisaged as an experiment to last for ten years, and there was to be no rate aid to pay wages to unemployed men. Instead, all money for the payment of wages was to be raised from voluntary sources. There were some other minor alterations as well, but these were the ones in which the working-class movements were vitally interested and the reaction was predictably hostile. The *Labour Leader* condemned the revision as 'the most indecent fraud ever perpetrated upon the working classes'.[74] Hardie, who said that the scheme was now an 'airy superstructure without any solid foundation', wasted no time in raising a petition signed by 7 lord mayors, 11 leading churchmen, 27 MPs, and 21 others including Lansbury and Alden, and calling for the government to resist outside pressures and pass the original Bill.[75] The Labour MPs were more divided than ever, for at a meeting held with the TUC's parliamentary committee on 24 July Hardie, Henderson and David Shackleton all joined Burns in opposing the new draft, even though the rest were still in favour of getting it through. Henry Broadhurst, the Lib-Lab member for one of the Leicester seats, and Crooks were among those who still supported the measure, Hardie later stating during the report stage that it was only respect for the latter's judgement that was preventing him from dividing against it when the vote was taken.[76] In spite of these divisions, however, the LRC had no intention of letting the agitation drop, as MacDonald explained in a letter sent to all the groups which had participated in the summer demonstrations:

I am instructed to say that the L.R.C. does not propose to allow the cause of the Unemployed to drop. So soon as we know what the purpose of the Government is exactly we shall consider plans for organising on a national scale an agitation to demand that something shall be done immediately on the lines of the resolutions on unemployment passed at our Liverpool Conference last January.[77]

The government's intentions were apparently made clear when on 31 July Balfour omitted the Unemployed Workmen's Bill from a list of those which were to be pushed through before the session ended. When challenged by Hardie he said that he had no intention of passing a Bill which included the rate aid clause, but without it the Bill's supporters did not seem very keen. At least, he added, he had received very little encouragement for the re-drafted measure.[78] But then, just as it seemed that the government had finally decided to let the Bill die, perhaps hoping to use labour's divisions as a further justification, there came the first sign of the uncontrolled violence which Hardie, for one, had already predicted as a result of the government's procrastination. A large group of Manchester unemployed, allegedly obstructing traffic in Albert Square, refused to disperse when ordered to do so and, inspired by Social Democrat agitators, rioted when the police made a baton charge on them. Hardie promptly sent off a telegram of congratulations, saying that the spirit of Peterloo was once more abroad in England and that now they would win their fight.[79] Certainly the incident produced a good deal of uneasiness in the press.

It was no coincidence that on 2 August, the day after the Manchester riot, the government began manoeuvres to withdraw from the difficult position in which it now found itself. A royal commission to investigate the poor law and the whole problem of poverty and distress was announced in reply to what Beatrice Webb later termed 'an evidently pre-arranged

UNEMPLOYED RIOTS.

SCENES IN MANCHESTER STREETS.

100 POLICE PRESENT.

MEN SCATTERED IN ALL DIRECTIONS.

THREE LEADERS ARRESTED.

Scenes occurred in Manchester this afternoon which have no parallel in the history of the city since the dreadful days of Peterloo, nearly a century ago. For some time now the unemployed have been agitating for the passing of the Unemployed Bill, now before Parliament.

Latterly they have been holding weekly and almost daily meetings in the Police Yard in Albert-street, but in order to bring their grievances more prominently before, and obtain the sympathy of, the public the venue was changed in defiance of the civic authorities. from the Police Yard to Albert Square. Several of these meetings have been held with no serious result other than a slight

In the meantime the unemployed made their way to Piccadilly, opposite the Queen Victoria monument. A rally was made, and Mr. Smith was amongst those who spoke.

When it became known that arrests had been made a large crowd of curious people (amongst whom were a few unemployed) assembled in Albert Square, and for a considerable time afterwards stood with their eyes on the front entrance to the Town Hall evidently awaiting further developments.

THE POLICE DENOUNCED.

At the Piccadilly meeting, the unemployed, who by this time were re-inforced by a large number of sympathisers, appeared to resent what one of them called "a gross interference with their rights." Amongst the most indignant were several women, who cried out what they would do to the police.

Several speakers addressed the meeting, and denounced the police for their conduct that day, a sentiment that was received with applause. Mr. Balfour and the Government came in for a share of the general indignation and when "boo's" were called for the right hon. gentleman a chorus of them was given lustily.

Threat To Rescue Prisoners.

One of the speakers, reverting to the occurrence, threatened that if any more arrests were made the unemployed in Manchester would not stop until they had succeeded in effecting their release. They would rescue them, he was heard to say amid the din, and "our comrades," he added, "we will stand by." The orator, who was hoarse with excitement, next appealed to the manhood and womanhood of the unemployed to assemble again in their fullest strength and to assert their right to free public procession and their

The Manchester unemployed riot. *Manchester Evening Chronicle,*
31 Jul 1905

question'.[80] Gerald Balfour's statement that the government was now anxious for the Bill to be tried as a three-year experiment contrasted vividly both with his own previous announcement that it was to last for ten years and with his brother's omission of it from the list of measures to be completed before the session ended. By 7 August the government had successfully steered the Bill through the Commons, resisting in the process two attempts by Hardie to reinstate the rate aid clause.

It was noticeable that during the debates the government speakers, particularly Arthur Balfour, stressed that the royal commission was part of a long-considered strategy. 'I have now to say . . . that, having given full consideration to the question,

we are of opinion that the time has now come when full inquiry . . . ought to be undertaken.' [81] But if the government
had been thinking about such a commission for some time,
why hadn't it been mentioned previously? The only evidence
to suggest that the government had thought about the matter
prior to 2 August 1905 consists of a letter written by Long to
Balfour—in December 1904. It was in reply to Balfour's query
as to how he should answer a letter from Herbert Samuel, the
Liberal MP, who had suggested that the government should
undertake just such an investigation. Long had replied that
there was much to be said for the idea, indicative again of his
real wish to tackle poverty and unemployment in a drastic
way, but had added that the present time was not suitable.[82] If
there had been any serious intention of setting up a commission it would have been a very useful foil against embarrassing
questions from labour deputations—but it was never mentioned. In February the Prime Minister had told Shackleton
that any tampering with the poor law would be a dangerous
thing.[83] On 9 May Gerald Balfour had said in reply to a
question from Hardie that the government had no intention
of setting up a small committee to examine the working of the
poor law.[84] In either case the announcement of a large-scale
inquiry would have done much to offset the unfavourable impression given by these essentially negative pronouncements.
Again, as late as 26 July the government had said that the Bill
was to be a ten-year experiment, though by 2 August it had
been reduced to three years, the natural corollary of a royal
commission whose report could reasonably be expected within
that time. 'Let us confess,' said the *Standard*, 'what ministers
will hardly deny, that the Royal Commission was an after-
thought suggested by the Parliamentary difficulty in which
they found themselves. . .' [85]

It seems clear, then, that the government, alarmed by the
ugly incident in Manchester, decided to resurrect a Bill which
it had virtually pronounced dead on 31 July, perhaps hoping

to offset some of labour's antagonism towards the new version by appointing a royal commission, an act which implied that once more information was available, a more far-reaching solution could be applied. In any case, Balfour must have known that, barring an electoral miracle, it would be a Liberal government which would have the task of putting the commission's proposals into effect. Nor was it unimportant that Balfour himself represented a Manchester constituency, and he may well have had one eye on his future election prospects. There was certainly no doubt in the labour press that he had 'been shaken by events in Manchester' and that the riot was directly responsible for the government's change of heart.[86] One trade union journal claimed that when the riot broke out 'hon. members suddenly developed a great anxiety to pass a Bill which but a short time previously they had in their own minds relegated to the House of Commons waste paper basket'.[87]

Even though Balfour had given in to the anti-Bill lobby and removed the rate aid clause, many labour writers and leaders still interpreted it as an acknowledgement of state responsibility for the unemployed, not now by extending the principle of local financial liability to its logical conclusion that the state was ultimately responsible, but deducing it from the simple fact that the government had legislated on the matter. This was the view of a writer in Robert Blatchford's *Clarion*, although he still termed the Bill a 'poor lopped off measure'.[88] When the dockers' leader, James Sexton, strongly attacked the bill at the TUC conference in September he was censured by the *Labour Leader*, which claimed that it was important because its very existence constituted an admission by the state of its duty towards the unemployed.[89] This same interpretation of the Unemployed Workmen's Act lay behind the decisions of both main socialist parties to insist that it be put into the fullest possible use in order to secure the practical recognition of the right to work. In addition, it was hoped that this would so exploit the measure's weaknesses that it would break down and prepare the way for a more radical scheme. Both the SDF and the ILP, therefore, took steps to organise the unemployed more effectively than ever before.

In August the ILP announced in a branch circular that a series of meetings would be held in leading industrial cities to consider ways and means of utilising the new legislation and also to enrol the unemployed in a permanent organisation pledged to secure the right to work. At the beginning of November, by which time most of these provincial conferences had been held and at least eight local 'right to work' committees already established, Hardie chaired a meeting of delegates from various labour and socialist groups to consider the formation of a National Right to Work Council. Originally it had been hoped that the LRC and the Labour MPs would carry out this task, but only Shackleton had turned up at the October meeting called to consider it. He had been against the launching of such a movement and it was therefore decided that it should be undertaken by the ILP.[90] Now in November a small committee was set up, charged with the job of drawing up a national manifesto and gathering funds. These developments were welcomed by the SDF in contrast with its hostile reception of the National Unemployed Committee in 1903. This favourable reaction may have been due to the fact that —unlike the National Unemployed Committee, which had been the brain-child of a radical, consisted of a Liberal-Labour alliance, and had had a very moderate programme—the new body was committed to a socialist objective and was entirely socialist in composition. George Barnes was the chairman, the treasurer was Lansbury, Frank Smith of the ILP was the secretary, while the committee members included Hardie; Pete Curran, of the gasworkers' union; Frank Rose, an ILP member of the Amalgamated Society of Engineers; Mary Macarthur, the women's labour organiser; MacDonald; Mrs Cobden-Sanderson, socialist daughter of the famous Richard

Cobden; and Harry Quelch. The inclusion of the last two may also explain the federation's support, for both were SDF members. By the beginning of December twenty-one local 'right to work' committees had been set up, and *Justice* was appealing for many more to be formed.[91]

A further explanation of the federation's friendly reception of the Right to Work Council was that it saw in it a means of making its own efforts more effective, even national, in scope. Working through the medium of the London Trades Council, the Social Democrats had secured the summoning at the end of September of a conference of London unions and socialist organisations. No representatives from the LRC were invited, although 96 trade unions, 4 ILP branches, the Fabian Society, and the SDF executive and London District Council all attended. It was agreed to set up the London Central Workers' Committee with the aim of co-ordinating agitation in the capital and establishing local committees in each borough to press the councils to put the new legislation into the fullest possible use. Just how far the SDF dominated this body can be seen from the fact that Quelch was elected chairman and that eight of the fifteen executive members were also Social Democrats—Knee, Harry Kay, John Hunter Watts, G. Patterson, Jack Williams, J. McLeod, T. Wall, and John Stokes. On 3 October the SDF contacted the ILP, suggesting that a national joint unemployment committee be formed to organise agitation on a national scale. The contents of the letter indicated clearly that the SDF had been greatly impressed by the success of the ILP-inspired demonstrations in the summer, which had compared very favourably with the federation's own efforts to organise a national demonstration in January. At this stage the ILP was still hoping that the 'right to work' movement would be organised by the LRC, and it was decided to urge the SDF to co-operate 'with that body'.[92] Just in case the LRC decided not to become involved, however, Hardie, Philip Snowden, and Bruce Glasier were authorised to act on behalf of the ILP in this matter. But there was evidently some disagreement about the attitude to be adopted towards the federation because only one of this trio, Hardie, later supported demonstrations organised by the London Central Workers' Committee in November and December. He was joined by Barnes and Smith, but it seems that Snowden and Glasier shared the view of MacDonald, who was totally against any co-operation with the Social Democrats. When they had first taken steps to set up the London Central Workers' Committee MacDonald had told the secretary of the ILP's metropolitan council that he had 'the best evidence for believing that the matter is only another SDF dodge to hamper the LRC'.[93]

But these efforts at organisation all received a considerable impetus when the Local Government Board eventually issued the orders for the new Act's administration. In addition to re-introducing several rules which had originally been dropped in response to labour pressure—for example, the regulation that a man could not receive work for more than two years in succession—each applicant was now required to fill in a very detailed personal record form. This, claimed Hardie, had the COS stamped across every page and unless an applicant could 'show the rudiments of angels' wings already in the sprouting stage, he or she may go hang for anything the act will do for them'.[94] When Gerald Balfour announced that nothing could be done about any of these unpopular regulations until the distress committees had been set up, both the SDF and the ILP campaigned vigorously for their own nominees. The Social Democrats were quite successful in London, and in West Ham secured no less than five places on the committee for SDF members. The ILP, too, managed to get some representation, scattered up and down the country, but in London the effort was bungled. MacDonald blamed Sanders, the party's London organiser:

So far as I can make out there are several nominations of
E

our kind of people few of whom know that the others are up. Now Sanders is paid to look after the interests of the I.L.P. in London and for his £50 he ought to put himself to the trouble of getting some unity imparted into our action. Instead things have been allowed to drift and once more the I.L.P. looks as if it were going to be out of it . . . it is all very sickening. . .[95]

Nor was the ILP-inspired Right to Work Council achieving very much. By the time Balfour resigned his premiership in early December it had only just managed to produce its manifesto. The London Central Workers' Committee, on the other hand, was extremely active. In one week alone, *Justice* claimed, the organisation had forced the Battersea Distress Committee to endorse the SDF's unemployment programme, led deputations to the authorities in Bethnal Green, Southwark, Hackney, Fulham, and Hammersmith, and had organised propaganda meetings in Kensington, Poplar, Paddington, and Westminster.[96] Large-scale marches through the West End were also arranged, particularly in November, and this campaign was so successful in keeping unemployment in the public eye that the *Daily Graphic* was forced to conclude that 'there is little chance of the London public being allowed to forget the Unemployed problem, even if they had a mind to'.[97] Others were less dispassionate. 'How long,' asked Sir Arthur Clay, 'is this sordid farce to be allowed to continue?'[98]

Balfour seems to have watched this socialist activity on behalf of the unemployed with a mixture of detached amusement and concern. In October he had been sufficiently interested to have his secretary draw up a report on its extent and objectives, but in November, probably encouraged by the downward trend in unemployment, he told the explorer and diplomatist, Sir Frank Younghusband, that 'it is curious that they should suppose . . . they can terrorise us into any such absolutely fatal admission as that it is the duty of the State to find remunerative work for everyone desiring it'.[99] He knew that the SDF was too small to present any real danger, and in any case the London Central Workers' Committee was running into financial difficulties of the sort which had always hampered the federation's work. At the end of November Fred Knee appealed for funds to support Jack Williams as a full-time organiser for the committee. It was again indicative of a new spirit of co-operation between the SDF and some members of the ILP that two of those who responded to this appeal were Hardie and Frank Smith.[100]

CHAPTER 3

The birth of the Right to Work Bill, 1906-1907

EARLY IN DECEMBER 1905 Arthur Balfour finally tendered his resignation to the King. This, said *Justice*, was no excuse for the labour movement to neglect the needs of the unemployed. On the contrary, the matter was all the more important because the past statements of the Liberal leaders, who were to form the next government, had not been very promising.[1] Certainly at various times during the previous three years they had come under heavy fire from labour and socialist writers for their failure to produce an unemployment policy. In November 1904, for example, Campbell-Bannerman had received a deputation of unemployed at Manchester and the *Labour Leader* had commented sadly that 'he could promise to do nothing . . . no opinions . . . no proposals . . . not even a programme'.[2] It is true, of course, that the party had established an unemployment committee late in 1904, but this did not produce any generally accepted policy, nor did it act as a stimulant to the Liberal rank and file. W. H. Beveridge, invited by Herbert Samuel in March 1905 to address a meeting of Liberal MPs on unemployment, gained the impression that his audience had not thought very much about the subject at all, and after the meeting was over C. P. Trevelyan, one of a group of Liberal members who were concerned that the party should have an advanced social policy, apologised to him for the lack of intelligence shown by those who had attended.[3]

Even as unemployment had got worse in 1905, and the government had at last introduced legislation, the Liberal leaders had only reluctantly taken a more active interest, and then mainly for political reasons. Gladstone had pointed out to Campbell-Bannerman that a short speech on the Unemployed Workmen's Bill 'would have a good effect and show that the Opposition takes a keen interest in the Bill'.[4] Similarly, in asking Buxton to move a resolution at a party meeting demanding permanent machinery to tackle the unemployed problem the Liberal MP, Augustine Birrell, stressed that 'it ought to be moved by a front bench man in order to prove our good faith and show that we mean *business*'.[5] But many remained unconvinced by the Liberals. In the *Labour Leader* 'Gavroche' noticed that at the height of the summer's unemployed agitation they were also holding demonstrations, but were not discussing unemployment. Although Liberalism had once meant something, he continued, it had now become a 'kind of lavatory where the parvenus tidy themselves up . . . before they pass in amongst the old nobility'.[6] Hardie, with some foresight, thought that even if the Liberals did intend to do anything for the unemployed once they were in power, there would be all sorts of party disputes, probably involving the House of Lords, and that as a result the unemployed would be forgotten.

Nor were these doubts about Liberal policies in any way modified once it became clear that Balfour's days at Downing Street were numbered. If anything they were increased when Edward Grey, soon to become foreign secretary in the new Liberal Government, said at Dudley on 15 November that the solution lay in education, land reform, housing and temperance legislation. This was followed by a vague statement from Campbell-Bannerman to the effect that 'whatever we do in the matter, I think it will be more deliberate and effectual than this', the reference being to the Unemployed Workmen's Act.[7] Still worse was to follow. At Walthamstow on 20 November another Liberal soon to enter the cabinet, John Morley, declared that he had no remedy at all. Not surprisingly, Campbell-Bannerman told Asquith shortly before Balfour resigned that 'much mischief was being done by the notion that we had little or nothing to say about the unemployed'.[8]

Much obviously depended on who was appointed to the Local Government Board and thus given responsibility for formulating a policy. When John Burns, famous for his role in the unemployed riots of 1886, was given the job it was not entirely unexpected, for in October 1904 one observer had advocated giving him this very post.[9] But Burns' views had mellowed greatly since his appearance at the Old Bailey in January 1888 on riot charges, and the news of his appointment went down badly with his former colleagues in the SDF. His old branch at Battersea issued a press statement claiming that his elevation was 'the crowning act and the reward of a whole series of betrayals of the class to which he belonged'.[10] Harry Quelch also took the view that Burns had received a fair reward for his apostasy.[11] But the less extreme sections of the working-class movement were not so critical. Hardie was cautiously—or, in view of his electoral pact with the Liberals, tactfully—optimistic. Trade unionists generally seem to have been pleased that a working man had at last found his way into the cabinet, and the clash of opinion between moderate and extremist was to some extent symbolised at a London Trades Council meeting on 14 December 1905 when Fred Knee opposed a motion applauding Burns' appointment. He was supported by all the SDF delegates and the resolution was declared lost when the voting went 37-37.

By and large, the first actions of the new government justified the attitude of those who were prepared to give it a chance. A circular, which came into effect in January, was issued from the Local Government Board in December, relaxing the regulation which had denied work under the Unemployed Workmen's Act to any who had previously been in receipt of poor law relief. The government was also thinking of increasing labour representation on the poor law commission. Although the TUC had petitioned Balfour for some representation, he had ignored its requests and when the names of the commissioners were announced at the end of November they were deemed sufficient, in the phraseology of one trade unionist, to send shivers of horror down the backs of all working men.[12] Only three, Lansbury, Beatrice Webb, and Charles Booth, were thought to be sympathetic to labour. The rest included C. S. Loch of the COS, Samuel Provis, permanent head of the Local Government Board, and charity workers Octavia Hill and Helen Bosanquet. The TUC evidently expected a friendlier attitude from the new Liberal administration, for on 20 December it decided to put forward the name of Francis Chandler, secretary of the Amalgamated Society of Carpenters and Joiners, and he was in fact added to the commission. Finally, although it was not public knowledge, a cabinet committee on unemployment was set up, consisting of Burns, Lord Ripon, Asquith as Chancellor, Gladstone as Home Secretary, and Sidney Buxton.[13]

Before this committee could work out any detailed proposals, however, the new government had first to face a general election. But it was no great ordeal, for it resulted in an enormous Liberal majority. Equally noteworthy for contemporaries was the emergence of the LRC which won 29 seats and almost immediately changed its name to the Labour Party. Many gloomy predictions appeared in the press about the policies which the new party would follow. As far as unemployment was concerned, one paper confidently forecast that it would compel the provision of work at public expense, which would, it was claimed, produce widespread pauperisation.[14] But in fact the Labour candidates themselves had suggested a remarkable variety of solutions for unemployment during the election campaign, and even after it was over they were frequently very vague when it came to putting forward concrete proposals.[15] Crooks, for instance, said merely that the Labour Party would take the matter up.[16] This lack of any clearly defined policy simply reflected the fact that the Labour Party had never previously been in a position to introduce detailed pieces of legislation. Notwithstanding the Liverpool unemployment conference of 1905, the Labour Party made its entry on to the parliamentary stage with no detailed programme on unemployment, only a general commitment to two principles: that each man had an inherent right to work, and that the state was financially and morally responsible for the unemployed.

Unemployment as such did not play a very important part in the election campaign and Liberal candidates frequently managed to get away with rather vague and imprecise expressions of sympathy for its victims, but little more. Generally, those who did have any constructive suggestions were advocates of land reforms, although there was some pressure from the party's radical wing for the establishment of national machinery or even the restoration of the original Bill of 1905.[17] After the election this radical group was augmented by newcomers such as Alden and G. P. Gooch. But even by the beginning of 1906 the government had not definitely made up its mind to introduce any unemployment legislation, for the Prime Minister told Asquith in a much-quoted phrase that 'two sops' for labour, a Trades Disputes Bill to offset the effects of the 1901 Taff Vale decision (which had made trade unions' funds liable for damages inflicted by their officials), and a Workmen's Compensation Bill, should be sufficient.[18] Lord Ripon, however, felt that it was imperative for the matter to be dealt with in the government's first session, and early in February the cabinet committee did in fact meet, and, according to Burns' diary, 'settled policy'.[19] When the new parliament assembled on 19 February 1906 it was informed that the Unemployed Workmen's Act of 1905 would be amended, although no details were given.

The labour movement reacted cautiously to this statement, and the Right to Work Council, determined to turn the many vague expressions of Liberal sympathy into something tangible, organised a massive public meeting on 21 February in the Queen's Hall, London, to remind the government that it was expected to honour its commitments. When in the middle of March Burns told Will Thorne, elected for West Ham South, that no day had as yet been fixed for the introduction of the amending Bill, the London Central Workers' Committee also arranged a demonstration in the East End which was addressed by the new Labour member for Sunderland, Tom Summerbell. But Burns steadfastly refused to commit himself and in May the Prime Minister refused to receive a deputation from the Right to Work Council. The response was another militant protest meeting, this time in Hyde Park, which was informed by another new Labour MP, James Seddon, that they would obviously have to 'strike the fear of man into the hearts of the Government'.[20]

Seddon was accompanied at this demonstration by Hardie, Barnes, and Thorne, but none of the other Labour MPs took part, much to the annoyance of Frank Smith. In a circular issued to all socialist bodies he proclaimed that the time for talking was over and that the Labour Party, to justify its existence 'must *act*'.[21] Accordingly, he then contacted MacDonald and asked him to summon a meeting of the Labour members to discuss what could be done to stimulate the government further. It was agreed to put heavy pressure on Burns in the Commons and questions were put by James O'Grady on 23 May, J. R. Clynes on 24 May, Thorne on 28 May, and Hardie two days later. This parliamentary attack was sustained during the Whitsun adjournment debate when Crooks joined Hardie and Thorne in protesting against the government's failure to redeem its promises. In the evening Henderson, Shackleton, and MacDonald presented the Prime Minister with a memorandum asking for a clear statement of the government's intentions. It had been signed by 115 Liberal and Labour members, a total which suggests that there was already considerable discontent with Burns' performance among the Liberal back-benchers. Indeed, only a few days before, one of them,

C. F. G. Masterman, had taken a deputation to see him and urge the necessity of immediate action on the unemployed question, but he had again refused to commit himself.

Burns' apparent lack of concern was all the more remarkable in view of the rising volume of dissatisfaction also expressed by the authorities responsible for the administration of the Unemployed Workmen's Act. The Glasgow Distress Committee condemned it as completely useless after only a few weeks, while in London the St Pancras Committee found the Central (Unemployed) Body far too slow in finding work for the applicants it recommended. Mrs Montefiore, the wealthy socialist who served on another of the London committees, in Hammersmith, later recorded her impressions of it.

> It seemed to me that the men who had formulated all unemployed schemes had veritably tried how not to do things. Long lists of men out of work were put before us week after week, and name after name was struck out as not being eligible.[22]

At its annual meeting the Association of Municipal Corporations overwhelmingly passed a resolution declaring that the present structure of the Act was unworkable.

Behind his mask of indifference, however, Burns was clearly being forced to do some rapid thinking as May drew to a close. His own cabinet colleagues were growing restless, Ripon telling Buxton that:

> It would be most foolish and even dangerous for the Government not to make provision before Parliament is prorogued for a possible want of employment next winter. I care little how it is done, but done it must be or we shall run a very serious risk.[23]

By the time this letter was written Burns had finally produced an idea, stimulated, it seems by Gladstone, Buxton and Ripon. Buxton told Ripon that:

> H. Gladstone agrees with us on an exchequer grant to
> tide the matter over temporarily. . . It is, I think, far the
> best temporary solution; and as Burns now proposes it
> himself it is a great thing gained to get him to . . . do
> something.[24]

But there was clearly some dissension within the cabinet, for
when the exchequer grant was discussed on 27 June Burns put
'my view, got my way'.[25] What had happened to the 'settled
policy' of February? What, in fact, had then been decided?

Conceivably, the cabinet committee had agreed to do nothing, pending the report of the poor law commission, although
this would mean that the statement in the King's Speech had
been completely misleading. It is true that the extensive
Liberal programme, which envisaged twelve major Bills, was
widely interpreted as a profession of faith rather than an indication of the practical possibilities for one session, but many of
the proposed measures were of an uncontroversial nature and
not expected to take up much time. Further light is thrown on
this question by Beatrice Webb, for shortly after the cabinet
committee meeting Burns had been to see her and she noted
in her diary that there was to be 'an amendment to the Unemployed Act of last session in the direction of great contributions from the rates'.[26] Now Burns had opposed the original
legislation of 1905 precisely because it had envisaged using
rate aid to pay the unemployed, and it is just possible that Mrs
Webb was mistaken. This, however, seems unlikely, if only
because the Prime Minister had informed Lord Knollys that
the amending Bill would 'have some of the features of the
original Bill of last year'.[27] It seems much more likely that
Burns had been over-ruled by his colleagues. He had thus
prevaricated about producing the amendment, which would
explain why *Justice* referred in March to rumours of ministerial splits over unemployment policy, and also why Burns'
own diary contains the following, oddly punctuated, entry for

12 May 1906. 'I do not like the Unemployed Bill to amend it is to extend the virtues of pauperised dependency and to inflict I am afraid a serious blow on the morale of the labourers ... presumably I am for resignation.'[28] His own preference, it seems, was to wait for the report of the poor law commission and he may have hoped all along that if it became necessary to do anything before the report came out he could propose an exchequer grant over which he could keep a tight control. Such a policy would certainly appeal to his departmental officials, the chief of whom was a member of the commission, and it would also appeal to labour, which generally believed that the Unemployed Workmen's Act should be financed from the exchequer. Either way, the differences of opinion within the Liberal cabinet committee had been brought into sharp relief by labour pressure, inside the Commons and in outside demonstrations.

The day after the cabinet finally accepted the proposal for an exchequer grant, Campbell-Bannerman informed the Commons that a full statement would be made on 19 July. But this was too late to prevent popular discontent manifesting itself. Early in July unemployed in Manchester, tired of the labour movement's inability to wrest anything from the government other than statements of future intent, seized a piece of church land and began to cultivate it. They were led by a man named Smith, who had been one of the Social Democrat ringleaders arrested in 1905 after the riot in Albert Square, and who now declared that 'this is the first battleground of a movement that will go down in history'.[29] His aim, he told an interviewer from *Justice*, was to draw public attention to the plight of the unemployed, to dispose of the popular myth that unemployed men were lazy, and to show the immorality of keeping land unused when it was the basic source of the necessities of life.[30] The SDF executive, perhaps impressed by Smith's predictions, but always eager to jump on to any likely bandwagon of discontent, sent Jack Williams to take charge of the Manchester men, and he dispatched a telegram to Burns reminding him of his stormy past. 'Manchester's unemployed have taken your advice of twenty years ago, and have gone back to the land . . . congratulate us.'[31]

Encouraged by his success, Smith next occupied a piece of land near Salford, but he was swiftly evicted by the irate owner. Williams, having established the Manchester men to his satisfaction, moved on to the 'Triangle Camp', which had been set up by a Social Democrat member of the West Ham Corporation, Ben Cunningham, on council property at Plaistow. This camp was short-lived, however, for Cunningham and his unemployed followers were evicted on 4 August after a short struggle with the police. His subsequent attempt to re-occupy the land led to his appearance in court. At Leeds the 'Libertarian Camp' only lasted for three days before hooligans broke in, turned out the unemployed occupants and burnt the tents. Perhaps the most successful of all was the camp organised by Albert Glyde of the ILP on land belonging to the Midland Railway Company near Bradford. By 25 August he estimated, probably very liberally, that 25,000 visitors had been to the camp and that over £50 had been raised by the sale of postcards and vegetables.[32] But these experiments in communalism soon came to an end as the various landowners asserted their rights and turned off their uninvited guests.

The general reaction had been one of tolerant amusement, although the National Right to Work Council had recommended the tactic and Thorne suggested that it might force the government's hand if carried out on a sufficiently wide scale.[33] But the SDF was just not strong enough outside London to organise such a movement, even if it had possessed the necessary financial resources, while most members of the ILP were still expecting the solution to come from parliamentary action, and even those in the National Right to Work Council were not prepared to involve themselves in extra-parliamentary pressure on such a scale.

Thus the government remained totally unmoved by these demonstrations of dissatisfaction, bolstered by the fact that some concrete proposals had finally been brought forward by Burns on 19 July. Burns had begun his speech with a survey of the current problem, asserting that as unemployment had many causes, so it had many solutions. This was why, he continued, the government had agreed to do nothing until the report of the poor law commission came out. In the meantime, a grant of £200,000, to be administered by the Local Government Board, was to be provided for the Unemployed Workmen's Act. Combined with rate money and voluntary subscriptions, this would make available something between £300,000 and £400,000. Legislation on small-holdings, crofters, and the army, all to be introduced shortly, would also make a contribution to improving the situation.

This statement was accepted on behalf of the Labour Party by MacDonald, who promised full support to the government. Although some of his colleagues criticised this action on the grounds that there had been no party meeting authorising him to do this, there can be little doubt that his action was a fair reflection of the views of most sections of the working-class movement. Will Crooks said that he approved of the government's proposals, while Barnes thought that 'an intelligent, if somewhat tardy, appreciation of . . . the problem has been evinced during the month'.[34] The railway workers' MP, G. T. Wardle, claimed that Burns' speech had been listened to with pleasure on the Labour benches.[35] It is true that neither *Justice* nor the *Labour Leader* were so enthusiastic, but it must be stressed that the programme only seems to have been accepted in the belief that the grant was a temporary measure. The railway servants' conference approved of it only 'as an instalment of what we anticipate in the near future'.[36] The editor of the engineers' magazine hoped for legislation in the 1907 session, seeing the £200,000 as a stop-gap.[37] A similar sentiment was evident at the TUC's September conference when the delegates, while agreeing that the sum was not enough, saw hope in the fact that this was the first time a government had ever made a national contribution to help the unemployed.

Thus when the TUC and the General Federation of Trade Unions (GFTU) both rejected a suggestion made jointly by the London Trades Council and the SDF early in 1907 that a demonstration be held to draw attention to those who were still out of work, their refusals were not due solely to the continuing prosperity of the economy—they owed much to the general labour expectation that the government would announce an unemployed programme in the King's Speech at the beginning of the session. This expectation also explains why the Labour Party, meeting in February to finalise the details of its own programme, decided to ballot for only four Bills, none of which had any direct bearing on unemployment. It was hardly surprising that when the Royal Speech concentrated entirely on the matter of constitutional relations between the Lords and Commons and made no reference at all to unemployment, the Labour MPs reacted angrily, and put down a censure motion on the government. Their resentment was well expressed by Clynes in a speech he made to the Commons in March.

> The £200,000 granted last year was surely not given in place of an amendment of the Act. He and his friends at least took it not as a sum which was to replace legislation, but as a sum to aid for some time pending a drastic amendment of the Unemployed Act in keeping with promises previously made by Ministers of the Crown.[38]

Immediately after the disappointment of the King's Speech, Hardie vowed that unemployment and old age pensions, also ignored, would be taken up vigorously by the Labour Party in the Commons, and little time was wasted in implementing his threat. The Joint Board, representing the Labour Party, the TUC, and the GFTU, met on 5 March and decided to appoint two sub-committees to draft reports and recommendations for an unemployed Bill. Hardie, MacDonald, Steadman, and John Ward, all MPs, were charged with the task of compiling the political sections, A. H. Gill (the MP for Bolton), Curran, Walter Hudson (who represented Newcastle in parliament) and Isaac Mitchell of the GFTU the economic parts.

The Labour Party's determination to produce this Bill must have been greatly increased when Burns, in reply to a question from the Labour member for Norwich, George Roberts, stated that he had nothing to say about renewing the exchequer grant and stressed again that he had no intention of amending the 1905 Act. He remained obdurate in the face of a rising tide of criticism about his administration of the Unemployed Workmen's Act and the exchequer grant. Many were annoyed by the petty nature of the regulations which he had added to the original legislation, and Hardie claimed that he had done a similar thing to the exchequer grant, hedging it round with so many restrictions as to make it virtually useless.[39] The same criticism was implicit in MacDonald's assertion, made at the ILP's Easter conference, that with a sympathetic administration the Act might have been 'a most valuable instrument'.[40] Burns was also attacked for breaking his pledges. In announcing the exchequer grant in July 1906 he had stated that the only condition for its use would be the degree of local distress, but it seems that in practice he had insisted on the locality making some contribution before he would sanction any allocation from the grant. This accusation was first made in a *Labour Leader* editorial and was then given more concrete form during an Easter adjournment debate in 1907 when Hardie cited Burns' refusal to give money to the Newport Distress Committee unless it raised funds locally as well.[41] Hardie said the knowledge that the government had set aside a large sum for unemployment relief would inevitably lead to a decline in the size of voluntary local subscriptions.[42]

The unwillingness of the Local Government Board to use any of the grant to finance experiments in relief also came under fire. Lansbury in particular attacked Burns' refusal to allow the Poplar Guardians to buy outright the land which Joseph Fels had leased them in 1904 with an option to purchase after three years.[43] Hardie informed the House of Commons that when the Glasgow Distress Committee arranged to buy land in order to start a farm colony, an arrangement sanctioned by an inspector from Burns' department, Burns himself had stepped in at the last moment to stop the purchase going through, even though the committee was planning to buy the land with money raised locally. He gave as his reason the imminence of the poor law report and the expiration of the 1905 Act, but in fact they were more devious than this.[44] He had always opposed labour colonies, noting after one visit to Hollesley Bay that it was 'a costly and foolish experiment developed by that prize fanatic G. L. . . . a holiday for 250 men from London . . . a process of coddling. . .'[45] He had never shared the view held by Lansbury and his supporters that farm colonies were a useful means of re-training men for future employment on small-holdings. As early as 1893 Burns had written in a Fabian tract that they were 'foredoomed to failure' being 'the revival in another form of the hated casual ward with all its physical and moral iniquities'. They were, he believed, unscientific, presupposing male labour, the absence of family ties, and only unskilled labour.[46]

His general reluctance to finance any experiment of this type was made much worse in labour eyes by the fact that he did not even spend all of the exchequer grant, much to the disgust of the Labour MPs who had generally thought it insufficient anyway. On 13 March 1907 Burns told the Commons that any remaining money would be returned to the exchequer at the end of the month. Two weeks later he revealed that well under half of the £200,000 had actually been spent, and Hardie seized on this during the Easter adjournment debate.

F

It was incomprehensible, he claimed, that with so much money left Burns had consistently refused to give more to schemes such as the workrooms set up in London to provide work for unemployed women.[47] It did little to enhance Burns' reputation that he was still holding so much of the exchequer grant when in February the Central (Unemployed) Body had been compelled to issue a public appeal for more funds.

By the beginning of June both the TUC and the GFTU had endorsed the reports of the Joint Board sub-committees and on 4 June the full board decided that a composite report in the form of a Bill should be forwarded to the Labour members and the trade union group for presentation to the Commons. After surveying the whole question of poverty the reports concluded that unemployment should be tackled in two ways. One was to try and secure the maximum number of workmen to perform such work as was required, the other was to increase the volume of available work, where it was advantageous to do so, in order to absorb surplus labour. The first of these objectives, it was argued, could be achieved by minimising fluctuations in the demand for labour by making time rather than manpower the elastic element in the labour-employment syndrome. The report thus urged all trade unions to make it official policy to abolish overtime working, or at least to restrict it as much as possible. In times of depression short-time working was advocated instead of the wholesale laying off of workers. The TUC had already been working along these lines, arranging conferences on overtime in accordance with resolutions passed at the Liverpool congress in 1906. The first of these had been held in March 1907 for workers engaged in engineering and shipbuilding, some 350,000 workers in these trades being represented by 40 delegates. They showed themselves keen to tackle unemployment by restricting overtime, but there were, as an observer from the National Amalgamated Union of Labour pointed out, many practical difficulties.[48] In June a second conference was held, this time for building-trade workers, and it passed similar resolutions dealing with the standard of wages, the legal restriction of overtime, and the need to establish a committee to coordinate efforts on these lines within the industry.

The second recommendation of the Joint Board report— that the volume of work should be increased where possible —was to be the function of the Bill which the parliamentary group was to prepare, but drawing it up was not without its difficulties. Will Thorne was opposed to the inclusion of any clause penalising those who refused work under the scheme, fearing that it would be harshly interpreted by middle-class administrators, but he was overruled and on 9 July 1907 Ramsay MacDonald took advantage of the ten minute rule to introduce the Labour Party's Unemployment Bill. It proposed the creation of a central unemployment committee to under-take the planning of national works and the appointment of local commissioners to develop and coordinate local works. Each local authority was to set up an unemployment commit-tee charged with the job of finding work for all registered unemployed in its area, and which could use rate money to pay men for any such work. The heart of the measure came in the third clause, embodying the principle of the right to work.

> Where a workman has registered himself as unemployed, it shall be the duty of the local unemployment authority to provide work for him in connection with one or other of the schemes herein-after provided, or otherwise, or failing the provision of work, to provide maintenance should necessity exist for that person and for those de-pending on that person for the necessaries of life.[49]

It was unfortunate from the Labour Party's point of view that the introduction of this Bill was completely overshadowed by the dramatic collapse in the Commons of the Liberal member for North Staffs, Sir Alfred Billson, who died shortly after MacDonald had resumed his seat. Although it was put down for a second reading on 16 July there was never any real chance of getting it further discussed. Government business had proceeded very slowly in the first half of 1907, owing to the obstructionist tactics of the House of Lords, internal problems within the cabinet, and the outpacing of administrative machinery by the sheer size and complexity of the government programme.[50] This had been appreciated by the Labour Party's strategists, and the Right to Work Bill, as it was soon popularly termed, had been introduced partly so that any weaknesses could be exposed and remedied, partly so that its principles could be well publicised by means of an intensive winter campaign in order to ensure that it would be familiar when it was re-introduced in 1908, the year the Unemployed Workmen's Act of 1905 expired. It would thus be a ready-made and well-understood measure which, it was hoped, the Liberal Government would be compelled to bear in mind when considering how to replace the 1905 legislation. When Parliament met in 1908, said Roberts, the Labour whip, it was anticipated that every party member would ballot for a day on which to bring in the Bill.[51] The *Labour Leader* warned that unless everyone combined to press the Bill upon the country's attention it would be 'obstructed, resisted and lost'.[52]

CHAPTER 4

The battle for the Right to Work Bill, 1907-1908

THE INTRODUCTION OF the Labour Party's Unemployment Bill did little to dent Burns' self-confidence. He condemned it as a prescription for 'universal pauperism' and did no more than renew the exchequer grant for one year, even then refusing to guarantee that it would all be spent.[1] In public speeches the Labour members kept up a constant sniping against his policies, and his obstinacy and growing unpopularity continued to alarm some of his cabinet colleagues, particularly when two socialists won by-elections at Colne Valley and Jarrow, in the last case, it was claimed, because of the candidate's advocacy of the Right to Work Bill.[2] In August Sidney Buxton, fresh from an interview with Burns, told Ripon that he had been able to

> extract nothing except that 'it is all going very well', which it is not (he will lose us all our seats in London if he's not careful)... It is important for us in our autumn speeches and before cabinets begin again to be able to say the Government intends to deal with the matter by *Bill* in view of the expiring of the act next year... I also want Burns to get pinned to something.[3]

The fears increased still more when the Labour Party's propaganda campaign got under way in July against a background of rising unemployment. Although the SDF had kept up local propaganda work in several cities, setting up a farm colony for Manchester's unemployed and raising over £170 for those in Hastings, the unemployed index had remained fairly steady at around 3.3 per cent in the first half of the year, but now its rise, coupled with an increase in commodity prices, indicated that the boom was coming to an end.

The campaign started with the publication in July of a pamphlet by MacDonald, who outlined the defects of the Unemployed Workmen's Act and its poor administration under the Liberals, and then gave details of the proposed new Bill.[4] In addition to this, 20,000 copies of the Bill were printed for general distribution and it was also printed as an official appendix to the party's July *Quarterly Circular*. The main thrust of the campaign, however, was embodied in a series of public meetings which took place in the autumn. By mid-September MacDonald already had 45 speaking engagements arranged for this purpose, Snowden 40, James Parker 12, and Tom Summerbell 8.

In undertaking this effort the Labour Party clearly had one eye on its position in the public interest, for Hardie told Bruce Glasier at some time during the summer that 'somehow we don't seem to bulk so large as we did in the eye of the public'.[5] It was hoped, too, to offset the growth of left-wing criticism which had grown up as a result of the party's failure to achieve anything in Parliament in 1907. Although old age pensions also featured in the speeches, unemployment held price of place and there was a militant tone in the voices of several of the Labour MPs. Summerbell told his Sunderland constituents that the party intended to fight to the death for the unemployed in the coming session.[6] Three weeks later at Nelson, Snowden said they would create such a wave of public feeling that the government would be compelled to legislate.[7] He spoke in similar vein at Maidstone and Chiswick in November and Rochdale the following month. At Newton, Seddon told his audience that if satisfaction was not forthcoming from the government in 1908 then 'wigs will be on the green at St Stephens'.[8]

Early in the new year Barnes brought out a pamphlet very

similar to MacDonald's, while Fred Jowett, MP for West Bradford, and the victor of Jarrow, Curran, took opportunities to stress yet again that unemployment would be the Labour Party's rallying call in the new session.[9] The ILP, too, was playing its part, the Metropolitan District Council organising a conference in January to keep all the London branches in touch with the latest developments and to discuss possible lines of action if the government again ignored the unemployed.

In a way the Labour Party's task was made easier by the continued deterioration of the labour market which produced an unemployment index of 5.8 per cent in the first month of 1908. Depression had set in, consequent upon a financial crisis in the United States and poor harvests in several countries. Unrest in Britain's industrial centres rose accordingly. Three major demonstrations organised by the London SDF in November and December 1907 had already produced some scuffles with the police and several arrests. Violent clashes occurred in Birmingham when in January Jack Williams arrived with a group of Manchester unemployed en route for London, and more arrests were made. Another Social Democrat agitator, A. P. Hardy, was arrested for obstruction when he tried to lead local unemployed into the King's seaside house at Brighton. Edward VII also figured in the plans of a third Social Democrat, Stewart Grey, who tried to present a petition to him. Informed by Gladstone that the King could not comply with its terms, Grey sent his followers to Brighton and took himself off to Windsor in order to fast in the chapel. Failing to achieve much by this gesture he moved on to London, announcing his intention of returning to Windsor at the head of an army of 10,000 unemployed.

The publicity campaign was successful in provoking critical observations about the Bill and several were forthcoming at a special conference assembled in January for the purpose of providing the renewed parliamentary struggle with a good send-off. W. C. Anderson of the ILP, for example, objected to the inclusion of a clause providing for the punishment of men who just refused work. Others were against the use of emigration as one of the remedies which the local unemployment committees could apply. Some wanted it made explicit that the scheme was only temporary, pending the transfer to collective ownership, but a resolution from the floor to insert such a clause in the Bill secured only thirteen votes. For the rest, MacDonald successfully defended the existing structure of the Bill, arguing that all members of distress committees agreed that it was greatly strengthened by the inclusion of the penal clause, and pointing out that emigration was not meant to be a general remedy, but simply one which could be applied in carefully considered individual cases. These points having thus been cleared up, the delegates unanimously passed a resolution approving the Bill.

With this backing the offensive was opened in Parliament by Arthur Henderson during the debate on the King's Speech, which had again ignored unemployment. He accused the government of raising false hopes and demanded to know why the Labour Party's Bill was not adopted if the government could not draft one of its own. The next day MacDonald, supported by Crooks, Snowden, William Brace the miner's MP, and Ward, moved an amendment regretting the omission of any unemployment proposals. But Burns still remained unmoved, claiming that their pessimism was unfounded, and stating that the government was preparing existing machinery for the implementation of the poor law report when it came out. According to the parliamentary correspondent of the *Labour Leader*, many Liberals pulled long faces when Burns went on to say that he would do no more than renew the exchequer grant for a further year, and back-bench discontent was certainly apparent when MacDonald was followed into the opposition lobby by 146 MPs, 70 of whom were Liberals.[10]

George Roberts declared that the support given to this amendment, which was followed four days later by the first reading of the Right to Work Bill, unchanged from its 1907 form, showed that the government could not ignore the matter much longer.[11] Certainly the press covered the debate very fully, all of the papers coming out strongly against the Labour amendment. This did not deter the party, however, from continuing its efforts to publicise the Bill, and early in February a circular was distributed suggesting that all labour organisations draw the attention of local MPs to its second reading, as it was 'desirable that Members of Parliament should be made aware of the interest which organised labour takes in the subject'.[12] This was followed by a second circular directly particularly at trade unionists, who in many cases seem to have been content to shelter from unemployment behind their own relief systems.

> What have you to say to the Bill? You know that the Unemployed man always threatens your wages. He increases the power of the non-Unionists. He is constantly liable to become a blackleg. He drains your funds. You have now to keep him whilst the man whom he enriches pays nothing... Wage Earners! Stand by the Unemployed and the Labour Party's Bill![13]

In provincial cities a series of successful demonstrations in favour of the Bill was organised, and the campaign culminated in London with a large public meeting on 12 March. It was addressed by MacDonald and Lansbury, and resolved to ask all the London MPs to be in their places the following day when the second reading debate was due.

The continuance of the labour pressure, the level of public interest, and the violence of unemployed agitation, obviously alarmed many Liberals, hence the large anti-government vote on 30 January. It is also significant that the first reading of the Right to Work Bill had been introduced by a Liberal radical, P. W. Wilson, as none of the Labour members had been lucky in the ballot. The Bill was deemed of sufficient importance to warrant a cabinet discussion on 11 March and it was apparent that the press rumours of ministerial divisions over the measure were well founded. Lloyd George was in favour of it.[14] Asquith told the King that the 'right to work' principle was 'obviously inadmissible', but felt that something should be done for the sake of appearances.[15] Buxton, too, thought that if the government was to oppose the Bill then 'we ought at least . . . to have an alternative'.[16] Lord Ripon, on the other hand, was not prepared to support it, believing that public opinion was not in its favour, but he did tell Buxton that he would not treat it too harshly.[17] Burns was completely opposed to it and left his colleagues in no doubt as to his views which he embodied in a cabinet memorandum. If the Bill was put into operation, he argued, no one would have any incentive to look for work, nor would any casual labourer take a temporary job unless it was well paid. Exaggerating in order to make his point, he went on to express doubts about the ability of an unemployment committee to find work simultaneously for 1,000 housemaids, 2,000 clerks, and 5,000 casual labourers. There was no reason at all, he concluded, to change the current policy of waiting for the report of the poor law commission.[18]

Birrell told a deputation from the Bristol Right to Work Committee that the principle underlying the Labour Party's Unemployment Bill might well 'mean the disruption of the Liberal Party' and it seems that he was not far from the truth, for the rank and file of the party was no less divided than the cabinet.[19] On the one side stood the radicals who had supported the 'right to work' amendment on the King's Speech; men such as Masterman, who was in favour of the government going 'forward boldly in some large and far reaching scheme of social reform'.[20] On the other wing were those like Harold Cox, the member for Preston, who thought that although the 'right to work' slogan was superficially attractive 'it is easier to advertise a quack medicine than to find a real remedy for a long-standing disease'.[21] The possibility of an embarrassing split over the Bill worried the Liberal whips a good deal and they prepared to take careful note of all those who voted against the government on the second reading. The Liberal whip, John Whitley, certainly did not mince his words. Each Liberal member was informed that 'an important division is expected. Your attendance and support of the Government is very earnestly requested.' [22]

So great was the interest generated by the Labour Party's campaign that many papers discussed the Bill's prospects in their morning editions, the *Mail* dismissing it as 'sheer insanity'.[23] The *Standard* published a series of short interviews with selected MPs, giving their opinions and voting intentions.[24] In spite of this interest, the House was little more than half full when P. W. Wilson rose to move the second reading on 13 March, and it seems that a good number of Liberals, including Lloyd George, had decided to escape their dilemma by absenting themselves from the debate, for they were not all paired. Wilson rather spoilt his opening speech by offering to drop the crucial third clause, and it is possible that this was the outcome of a visit he had recently made to Asquith, who was acting head of the government as Campbell-Bannerman was ill, and who wanted to do something, but opposed the 'right to work' principle. Certainly several Liberal members might have voted for the measure had it been made less controversial in this way, but it hardly mattered, for MacDonald, who was seconding, immediately contradicted Wilson by affirming that the Labour Party was not prepared to omit the clause.[25] The government put up two members with trade union interests, Fred Maddison and Henry Vivian, to oppose the Bill, and both claimed that it would create more unemployment than it relieved, arguing strongly that it was the fruit of socialist agitation and not wanted by the trade union movement. This allegation hardly accorded with the way in which the Bill had been drawn up, and it provoked the anger of the miner, Brace, certainly no socialist, who promptly rose

PARLIAMENT AND THE PEOPLE.

EXCITING DEBATE ON THE UNEMPLOYED.

MR. JOHN BURNS BURNS HIS BOATS.
CABINET TROUBLES.

BY OUR OWN CORRESPONDENT.

Friday was a regular field-day. Never before has the House been so thoroughly roused on the occasion of a Labour debate. Never have the chiefs of verbal warfare thrust and parried with a keener edge. At a culminating crisis of the fight Will Crooks arose, flushed and excited, and said of one of Mr. John Burns' characteristic misrepresentations: "It's speech effective enough. It had very little reference to the Bill, and every second or third sentence was diversified by some reference to the fiends called "Socialists"; but the House roared with laughter at many of his references. "I have never had such a lapse in my reason as to become a Socialist," he confessed; and the House evidently believed him.

The Right to Work Bill debate. *Labour Leader*, 20 Mar 1908

to announce that he had not intended to participate in the debate but he wished to state categorically that trade unionists did support the measure.[26] And so, after a lengthy debate, did a good number of Liberals, for when the vote was taken 116 votes were recorded in favour of giving the Bill a second reading. The magnitude of this rebellion again produced considerable alarm. One anti-socialist stated that the introduction of 'this astounding measure . . . from the Liberal benches is pregnant with warning'.[27] The hysteria which afflicted the Conservative press was well illustrated in the *Telegraph's* comment that 'whoever supports the bill is a socialist and ought to wear a red flag as an outward sign of his being a dangerous firebrand'.[28]

With public interest running at such a high level the Labour Party was in no mood to abandon the struggle, and shortly after the debate on the second reading was concluded the order for the second reading of an Eight Hour Bill was read and withdrawn. This Bill had originally been introduced on 11 February by Will Thorne at the request of the TUC

and was down for a second reading on 1 May. It was withdrawn, however, because Pete Curran, successful in the draw
for a day on which to discuss a parliamentary motion, decided
to bring one forward on the eight-hour day. According to the
procedural rules of the Commons, he could not do this when
a Bill on the same topic was still before the House. As his
motion was to be discussed on 18 March it seems that Thorne's
Bill was dropped so that Curran could use the opportunity to
press home the unemployment attack. From the point of view
of publicity he was fairly successful, for there were several
press comments on the discussion, a typical one labelling the
idea as a 'fresh challenge to the country's common sense'.[29] But
the Labour spokesmen did not really make the most of this
opportunity, failing to stress that an eight-hour day would
effectively increase the amount of available work and thus
answering those critics of the Right to Work Bill who had
claimed that the measure gave no indication of how the guaranteed work was to be provided.

It was claimed that the Labour Party's campaign for the
unemployed had been so successful that the government dared
not ignore the problem much longer, and MacDonald told an
audience at Halifax that they would not allow the problem to
sink over the horizon again. But what was to be done before
the next session when the Bill could be brought in again? At
a meeting of the Joint Board held on 17 and 18 March it was
decided to persist with the efforts to keep the measure before
the public.

> The appeal must now be made to the country. At tens of
> hundreds of Socialist meetings during the year the de-
> mand that the Bill be passed must be made, and at every
> meeting in the constituencies addressed by members who
> voted against the Bill their action must be challenged.[30]

In a word of general encouragement to all those who had
joined in the campaign, MacDonald, enclosing copies of the

division list, asserted that there was no intention of letting the principle drop, and he urged everyone to persist with the education of the electorate. The second thread of Labour's future policy was to defend the Bill against those who were misrepresenting it, both in the press and at public meetings. A special pamphlet was issued explaining certain clauses which had been subject to uninformed criticism, particularly clause three, and another circular was prepared stating that the Joint Board repudiated 'most strongly the suggestion that in its working it will be inimical to Trade Unionism'.[31] A policy of this sort was certainly necessary because Liberal politicians especially seem either to have misunderstood the scheme or, more likely, deliberately misrepresented it. There were some, such as the old-school radical H. J. Wilson, who genuinely disliked the Bill, but others seem to have purposely distorted its probable effects. Churchill, for example, said at Dundee that it would entitle a man to claim work 'no matter how bad his character'.[32] Walter Runciman, recently made President of the Board of Education, claimed during the by-election at Dewsbury that

> Any workman out of work for any cause, good, bad, or indifferent—for incompetency, for insobriety, for laziness —could come to the Dewsbury local authority and . . . if they said 'We have no work to give you', he could reply, 'Then you must maintain me and my family.' I venture to say that such a bill would put a premium, not on the best, but on the worst, of our working classes.[33]

Even Lloyd George, speaking in support of Churchill at his Manchester by-election, now proclaimed that the measure was a bad one, his change of heart almost certainly being connected with his recent promotion to the exchequer, which would have had to find the money had the Bill become law.

This spate of by-elections was produced by the ministerial changes made by Asquith when he took over the post of prime minister from the ailing Campbell-Bannerman in April. It is a further indication of the government's embarrassment over the Right to Work Bill that Asquith apparently decided to use this cabinet shuffle as an opportunity to remove Burns from the Local Government Board. At least, this was one of the offices which he offered to Churchill, and even when it was refused in favour of the Board of Trade it was on the understanding that unemployment should now be tackled in the long term from this department.[34] One of Churchill's first actions in his new post was to take on Beveridge and begin the planning of a national system of labour exchanges. Asquith, having in this way bypassed Burns' responsibility for a long-term unemployment policy, then contented himself by sending Masterman, by now very much the radical confidant of Lloyd George and Churchill, to the Local Government Board as Under Secretary in the hope of offsetting the President's conservatism. Burns was apparently none too keen on this arrangement and wrote hastily to Asquith.

> I am not sure . . . whether you have finally decided upon the proposed colleague you mention. . . If not then I should like a word with you first. If you have decided I will of course receive in a friendly spirit any man you may consider desirable to send here.[35]

He was too late, however, for Masterman got the job, having made it clear that he expected Provis to be replaced by someone with a drastic mandate for reform.[36] It was perhaps indicative of Burns' weakened position that when Sir Berkely Sheffield asked on 23 June whether the government intended to renew the exchequer grant for a further year, the question was answered by Masterman, who said that the matter was being discussed by Churchill and Lloyd George.

The development of some new, long-term unemployment policy, implied by these ministerial changes, was every day becoming more urgent as the depression deepened. By June the unemployed index had risen to 7.9 per cent and violence broke out in several cities. Windows were smashed in Manchester in protest against the government's inactivity, while in Glasgow workers from over forty trades took part in a massive anti-government demonstration at the end of June. But working-class discontent was not directed solely against the government, for many voices were raised against the apparent quiescence of the Labour Party which, apart from one attempt, voluntarily abandoned, to prevent the Unemployed Workmen's Act being included in the Expiring Laws Continuance Bill, had remained strangely quiet since March. In Parliament its attentions were concentrated on the Old Age Pensions Bill, and leaders such as Henderson and Shackleton were also very interested in the fate of the Licensing Bill.

This lack of vigour in Parliament and the necessary but unspectacular policy of educating the electorate about the Right to Work Bill combined to create the impression that the party had forgotten the unemployed. At the ILP conference in April one delegate advocated that obstructionist tactics should be used in the House of Commons in order to force the government's hand.[37] In July the Yorkshire Federation of Trades Councils added its voice to the growing volume of criticism, perhaps taking its cue from J. M. McLachlan, a member of the ILP, who had condemned the Labour Party for following a policy of political opportunism and modest palliatives.[38] The Social Democrats, too, who had welcomed the appearance of the Right to Work Bill and encouraged the party's campaign in the winter of 1907-8, were now highly critical of the party's failure to force it through Parliament by militant means. Two members of the Fleetwood Branch suggested that each local organisation should send postcards to all the Labour MPs asking them to drop all other matters. 'Practically nothing,' complained *Justice*, 'is being done. . . The Labour Party in the House of Commons seems to think that it has done its duty.'[39] Even the *Labour Leader* was moved to admit in August that the party had not managed any 'striking performance from a popular point of view'.[40]

This dissatisfaction was not confined to the party's left-wing critics or even its own non-parliamentary members, for the seemingly apathetic policy followed after the defeat of the eight hours resolution and its failure to make any significant impact also disturbed some of the MPs who had constantly pressed the cause of the unemployed since the election of 1906. The parliamentary pressure of that year, the militant speeches of the 1907-8 campaign, and the bombardment of the government benches in 1908 had been very largely the work of a certain number of Labour MPs—MacDonald, Snowden, W. T. Wilson, Henderson, Crooks, Thorne, Jowett, Seddon, Charles Duncan, Curran, James Parker, T. F. Richards, Hardie, Barnes, O'Grady, Clynes, Roberts, and Summerbell. Now the discontent of some of this group was implicit in the re-convening of the National Right to Work Council in London on 31 July 1908, the day that the parliamentary session ended. The council had been silent since the middle of 1906, mainly because its members had put their faith in a parliamentary policy focused on the Right to Work Bill. The failure to achieve anything in this way and the ensuing disappointment among some of these 'activists' clearly lay behind this meeting, and the executive now decided to collect reliable statistics from the main industrial cities and also to invite trades councils and other working-class organisations to form local committees in order to carry out a winter agitation. By the middle of November Frank Smith had circularised 1,500 trade unions, 250 trades councils, and 1,400 socialist societies, urging them to exert pressure to secure the early re-opening of the distress committees, asking how many men had been on short time during the year, and asking trade unions to state how many of their members were out of work in the third week of September. At least eight, and possibly as many as twenty-five new committees came into existence in response to this appeal from Smith (see Table 2, pages 191-2). In order to strengthen

G

the campaign in London the Right to Work Council also contacted the ILP's Metropolitan Council, asking it to form a
special sub-committee to organise the work, but the council
decided instead to refer the matter to the executive with the
suggestion that all the London branches simply be asked to
release their organisers for two weeks from 11 September,
when the campaign was due to get under way, for special work
with the unemployed. It seems from this that the Right to
Work Council envisaged the London ILP filling the role
played in 1905-6 by the now defunct Central Workers' Committee.

These preparations were assisted to a considerable extent by
the failure of the labour market to recover during the summer
months. By August 8.5 per cent were out of work, and as the
winter approached the unemployed grew still more militant.
In September 200 Glasgow unemployed broke into the council chamber and forced the commencement of several relief
schemes. Two days later they interrupted Prince Arthur of
Connaught as he was inspecting a Glasgow company of the
Boys' Brigade, and then interfered with a civic lunch at which
he was guest of honour by singing the 'Red Flag' outside the
town hall and shouting imprecations against the royal family.
The situation looked so bad at one point that troops in the
nearby barracks were alerted. In Manchester the police, as in
1905, resorted to baton charges to break up a gathering of
unemployed in Stevenson Square, and one of the ringleaders,
a man named Skivington, subsequently led a large number
of the crowd into the cathedral where they punctuated the
sermon with comments. Skivington was only prevented from
seizing the pulpit by a quick-thinking organist who drowned
his attempts to address the congregation. A silent gathering of
some 10,000 unemployed outside the Sheffield town hall so
unnerved the councillors that £10,000 was promptly voted for
relief works. From Nottingham 150 men set out to march to
London, and elsewhere in the Midlands there were clashes

between unemployed and the police. On 4 October, Stewart Grey, who had been leading hunger marchers from city to city, was arrested in Trafalgar Square for obstruction. He was twice rescued by the mob and twice re-captured by the police.

These signs of violence alarmed many who saw behind them the influence of the socialist agitators. 'It is gratifying to learn,' ran one account, 'that the worst excesses are due, not to the distress of starving people, but to the deliberate policy of the Socialist Party.' [41] The editor of the *Express*, Ralph D. Blumenfeld, had already taken steps to formalise the structure of the Anti-Socialist Union, and by the autumn he was issuing constant warnings about the increasing influence of socialism. But there were also those who encouraged the violence. Victor Grayson told the unemployed not to stay in their hovels but to

> come out . . . and to thrust their pinched starved faces into the faces of the well conditioned multitudes . . . they would be less than men if they did not use what energy this cursed civilisation had left them to get food immediately.[42]

A writer in A. P. Orage's *New Age* claimed that the Glasgow riot had been the best protest achieved by the unemployed.[43] Even at the TUC the advocates of violence were heard, one Social Democrat delegate claiming that they had to strike the fear of man into the hearts of the ruling classes and that little would be secured while the Labour MPs were content to remain so respectable.[44] Will Thorne told one of his audiences to help itself from the bakers' shops if it was short of bread, advice which resulted in his prosecution for incitement. The Social Democratic Party (the Social Democratic Federation had adopted this new title late in 1907) was also encouraged by this spread of unemployed militancy and decided to try and channel it more effectively by setting up small committees on lines similar to those of 1886 and 1903. Since 1905 the Social Democrats had been comparatively quiet about unemployment, partly because it had not been sufficiently serious to work on very effectively, as the fiasco of land-grabbing in 1906 had shown, and partly because the focus of attention had passed to the Labour Party and Parliament. Even if they had wished to encourage agitation on a wide scale, financial stringency would almost certainly have stopped them. The London Central Workers' Committee had collapsed in 1906 for want of funds, and although Jack Williams had organised daily meetings at Tower Hill and the occasional demonstration he had been working for nothing by March 1907, as the executive could no longer afford to pay him. During the same year it had been necessary to consider raising members' subscriptions, and in the spring Knee had had to report that the London Organisation Fund was 'absolutely bankrupt'.[45]

On 19 September 1908 the London branches of the Social Democratic Party (SDP) set up a central committee to run the agitation, but things did not improve financially, and the party's hopes of fomenting unrest in the provinces were dashed by the poor response to an appeal made for money to finance it. The London effort would probably have failed as well had it not been for the generosity of Lady Warwick, who contributed £40 of the £42 4s 6d (£42.23) raised by the middle of October.[46] The first stage in the London campaign was a demonstration in Trafalgar Square on 10 October, and the threatening slogans on the marchers' banners certainly lived up to Quelch's warnings that their aim was to 'make the unemployed a menace . . . institute a reign of terror . . . make the governing classes howl with affright at the danger to their skins and their stolen wealth'.[47] Will Thorne, who addressed the meeting, again appealed to his Labour Party colleagues to obstruct all legislation until unemployment had been dealt with. Two demonstrators were arrested. It was in this sort of atmosphere that Parliament re-opened on 12 October, the suffragettes adding their contribution to the scenes of violence in Parliament Square. The Right to Work Council had already been organising street demonstrations as well, and some idea of the strain which this agitation helped to impose on the capital's forces of law and order can be seen in a letter received by Gladstone on 11 October.

> Henry [Commissioner of the Metropolitan Police] said that the strain on the police caused by demonstrations of women, unemployed, etc., was heavy and was increasing. Yesterday or Thursday (I forget which day) he had 'hunger marches' taking place in *twenty* divisions. Every march had to be accompanied by a body of police: otherwise they would have begun to break into shops.[48]

Church parades were organised on the morning of 11 October, followed by public meetings in the afternoon and evening. Each meeting, held under Right to Work Council and ILP auspices, appointed deputations to wait on the London MPs on the first day of the autumn session, and when these deputations began to arrive at about six o'clock in the evening considerable pressure was put on the police, some 2,500 of whom were packed around the Houses of Parliament. Several of the Labour Party 'activists' supported the requests of the deputations to meet their respective MPs, who were eventually informed by the police that if they did not receive them, there would be a full-scale riot.

This autumn sitting of Parliament had been called by the government in order to complete the passage of outstanding items of legislation, particularly the Licensing Bill. But the rise in the numbers out of work and the spread of violence meant that the cabinet, further stimulated by Labour demands in Parliament for some statement of its intentions, was almost immediately plunged into discussion about the unemployment situation. On 14 October Burns was informed, somewhat abruptly, that something had to be done straight away, and a small committee consisting of L. Harcourt, the First Commissioner of Works, Churchill, Lloyd George, Reginald McKenna,

Gladstone, Buxton, and Burns himself, was established to draw up a list of proposals for immediate implementation.[49] The same day Asquith announced that he would make a full policy statement the following week. It was either a tribute to the Labour Party's pressure or an indication of Liberal poverty that the Labour Party chairman was called in to give advice. Henderson was well aware of the feelings of some of his colleagues, for on 16 October he warned the cabinet that unless prompt action were taken he would be unable to restrain his extremists.

In fact, one parliamentary extremist, Grayson, had already shown his displeasure on the previous day, leaving the House in disgust when the Speaker ruled that the Licensing Bill must take precedence over his motion for an adjournment in order to discuss the plight of the unemployed. On 16 October he was suspended when he tried to interrupt the committee stage of the same Bill, and as he was being escorted from the Commons he turned and loudly condemned the Labour Party as a traitor to its own class. Grayson, however, was not a member of the Labour Party, having won Colne Valley without its official backing. In warning the cabinet about his extremists, therefore, Henderson must have had in mind somebody else, and it seems that his concern was about a small group of the 'activists' which, as well as working vigorously in Parliament for the unemployed, had also co-operated actively with the Social Democrats on several occasions. Hardie, Seddon, and Thorne, for example, had all supported the 1906 demonstrations held jointly by the Right to Work Council and the London Central Workers' Committee, while Curran and Thorne had both given their support to the tactics of the land-grabbers in the same year. Thorne and O'Grady had both attended the SDF's major protests of 1907 in London, and Roberts, Summerbell, and Thorne again had all appeared at some of Jack Williams' Tower Hill meetings.[50] At least two of this group sympathised with Grayson's action, disagreeing only with its timing. Thorne told his union executive that he would have acted with Grayson had the Labour Party not already agreed to wait for the government's policy statement.[51] Fred Jowett said that although neglecting one's duty and then expecting to make up for it by 'theatrical display' was not war, he would 'make one of a number to court suspension or anything else which would be likely to cause confusion in the ranks of the enemy' if the government's proposals weren't satisfactory.[52]

Now on 19 October this small group, led by Hardie, attended a joint meeting with the SDP's London unemployment committee, and agreed to set up a Joint London Right to Work Committee with the Social Democrat, E. C. Fairchild, as secretary, in order to bring greater cohesion into the London agitation. Hardie had clearly decided that, to be effective, any parliamentary effort really needed the backing of some militant outside pressure. Such pressure was bound to be more effective, both morally and physically, if led from the capital where the SDP was stronger than the ILP and had already organised a successful network of unemployment committees, whereas the ILP's London council had been reluctant to do more than place the various branch organisers at the disposal of the Right to Work Council. That the Social Democrats were prepared to work with members of a party which they had been criticising since 1907 is explained in part by the fact that some of them were still hoping to form a united socialist party, and the 'right to work' slogan was one which they could heartily endorse. Significantly *Justice* said in announcing the formation of the Joint Committee that 'we have entered into active co-operation with the National Right to Work Council and we hope in that, as in other directions, to render effective service to the unemployed *and socialism*' (my italics).[53] Then there was the undoubted attraction of being involved in a national movement, their own efforts at organising on this scale earlier in the autumn having failed miserably. Finally, of course, there was the perennial problem of finance which the National Right to Work Council with its wide trade union support could reasonably be expected to avoid.

Clearly, however, the use to which Hardie and his friends put this new London organisation depended largely on the contents of the government statement. But the cabinet was not finding it easy to make up its mind, and while Hardie negotiated with the Social Democrats, Henderson continued to negotiate with the government. His suggestions that the exchequer grant should be increased and that rate money should be used by local authorities to pay wages to men employed under the terms of the Unemployed Workmen's Act were favourably received by Churchill, Masterman, and Buxton, but were fiercely denounced by Burns in a cabinet memorandum. All he would concede was an increase in the size of the exchequer grant—if it was really necessary—relaxation of some of the regulations issued for the administration of the 1905 Act, and a few other administrative changes. The poor law report was imminent, he claimed, and he could see no reason to change the policy of waiting for its suggestions, especially as it would require legislation to enable the local authorities to pay wages out of the rates.[54] Three days passed before the cabinet eventually resolved its differences and it was Burns who triumphed having, in his own words, 'made a dogged fight. W.C. and L.G. fought equally hard but wore them down by weight of mettle. At end L.G. capitulated and urged economy for Treasury's sake.'[55] The same night Asquith informed the King of the government's plans and it was clear, as Mrs Masterman recorded, that 'J.B. has scored all along the line, partly because he came armed with figures . . . partly because the distrust of the Ll.G.-Churchill combination is so profound in the Cabinet'.[56]

Asquith introduced the government's proposals on 21 October, prefacing his remarks with the comment that he could not anticipate any of the measures to be introduced next session, a thinly veiled reference to Churchill's labour exchange scheme.

For the present it was proposed to increase the exchequer grant to £300,000, to relax some of the regulations pertaining to the Unemployed Workmen's Act, and to provide an extra 24,000 places in the army's special reserve. In addition, Admiralty orders for warships were to be brought forward and repair work in Admiralty shipyards was to be speeded up. Finally, over 8,000 men would be given temporary employment over Christmas in the Post Office. All this, noted Burns with some satisfaction, was a 'real triumph' as the Labour Party had been completely out-generalled over the question of the penny rate.[57]

It was reported in the press that the Labour Party's trade union section was generally satisfied with this programme, although the whole party did back a motion disapproving of it. But when a vigorous offensive of questions, lasting through the rest of the session, was mounted it was noticeable that it was conducted almost entirely by the 'activists'. This campaign concentrated on two themes: the problems of areas where distress committees did not exist, and aspects of the programme which, it was felt, could be extended. According to one report, the aim of this attack was ultimately to swamp Burns' department and cause him to spend all the exchequer grant by Christmas.[58] This was probably an exaggeration, but certainly at the beginning of November MacDonald contacted all local authorities drawing their attention to the effect of Asquith's statement and urging them to secure for their own unemployed a share of the promised relief. He wrote to ILP branch secretaries, too, asking if their local council had applied for permission to form a distress committee and also asking for specific information about local needs.

The parliamentary questions began as early as 27 October when Snowden asked Burns if the authorities at Keighley had requested permission to create a distress committee and with what result.[59] This was the first of a series of such queries, always couched in exactly the same terms, which were put regularly during the autumn session until 3 December when the climax—eight questions in one sitting—was reached. At intervals the Labour members asked for statements about the number of successful applications, and eventually Burns admitted that 52 had been made altogether of which he had sanctioned 14 only. Questions were also raised about areas too small demographically under the regulations of the 1905 Act to have committees. On 11 November Summerbell asked if grants would be made to these areas if they set up their own special committees, but was told that they did not qualify.[60] The same day Hardie asked, unsuccessfully, if the extra £100,000 promised by the government could be provided on conditions which would permit its use by these deprived districts.[61] Curran then suggested on 13 November, again without success, that such areas should be combined and one committee formed for the whole.[62] Ten days later, Hardie repeated his plea for the extra money to be made available to places which did not qualify for the original grant, but was again informed that this was not possible.[63] A second theme of this questioning concerned particular aspects of the government's plans. Thus Richards asked Burns if he would circularise the distress committees with advice about the best sort of work to provide for the unemployed.[64] George Roberts wanted to know how many people had been induced to emigrate by the distress committees.[65]

The most sensational incident springing from this constant pressure on Burns came on 12 November when, in reply to a question from Thorne, he stated that his recently issued circular concerning the removal of restrictions on applicants for work allowed full discretion to local distress committees to relax such barriers. Henderson immediately rose and asked if this was what Asquith had meant in his statement of 21 October, and later in the day he moved the adjournment of the Commons in order to draw attention to the discrepancy between the Prime Minister's promise and Burns' circular. The

covering letter which Burns had sent with the new order,
alleged Henderson, completely contradicted Asquith's own
declaration. Asquith replied that Henderson was quite correct
in supposing that he had not meant to imply simply that the
local committees should have a discretionary power, but that
the restrictions should be lifted entirely. He had talked the
matter over with Burns and the error had now been rectified.[66]
This public rebuke clearly upset Burns and he noted with
almost poetic sadness, that 'I sat serene and endured the spleen
but wondered for its source. . . An unexpected blow from the
P.M. Why?'[67]

The 'activists', faced with this repeated resistance from
Burns, made one final effort in Parliament before the session
ended. Hardie brought in a two-clause Bill on 8 December
which would have amended the 1905 Act to allow local authorities to pay wages from the rates, and which would also have
given the status and power of distress committees to the
smaller bodies created by the Unemployed Workmen's Act to
collect statistics and run labour bureaux in districts too small
to qualify for full committees. Hardie hoped that the government would take up his measure and it was put down for a
second reading the following day. But the session was nearly
over and it never came up for further discussion. It was evident at a Joint Board meeting held on 9 December that in
introducing this Bill, Hardie had been acting on his own
initiative, almost certainly on behalf of the 'activists'. He had
to explain that his action had in no way been meant to reflect
on the status of the Board.[68]

Meanwhile, the SDP had begun to implement the street
campaign in the form of marches into the West End. Williams
was put in charge of this, and he led the first procession of
some 2,500 men through London's richer quarters on 25 November. Shopkeepers promptly began to complain, as they had
done in 1903, and their anger was doubtless exacerbated when
so many men turned out on 16 December that Oxford Street

was completely blocked. Two days previously a question had been asked in the Commons about the possibility of increasing the strength of the London police force in view of 'the great increase of duties recently thrown upon it'.[69] Similar disquiet was apparent when, shortly after Christmas, another Social Democrat organiser, R. Greenwood, began to hold a series of unemployed meetings in the fashionable West End squares. Grosvenor Square was the scene of one such demonstration on 13 January, and a second, held the following week in Belgrave Square, was the occasion of much violence. Typical enough was the case of Joseph Lloyd, arrested for inciting people to attend these gatherings armed 'not with your fists but with something else'.[70] One protester claimed that the only object of these meetings was to insult West End residents.[71] Others feared that only the police stood between London and total riot.[72] Thus it was not surprising that the police resolved to take a much firmer stand in the future, and permission was refused for a second meeting in Belgrave Square which Green-wood had planned for 25 January.

At first sight, then, the alliance between the National Right to Work Council and the SDP was working well, an intensive parliamentary campaign being supported and then sustained over the Christmas recess by street agitation. But when, early in February 1909, the Joint London Right to Work Committee asked the Labour MPs to support a demonstration being arranged to coincide with the opening of Parliament all but O'Grady refused. When this demonstration ended in a rowdy fiasco Barnes firmly denounced it in the House of Commons, saying that while he was glad that 'the sea of suffering surging round our very doors . . . last night even, overflowed into our lobby', he wished to dissociate himself from people who organised great demonstrations and then failed to make adequate provision for those taking part. 'We had nothing to do with that, and will not have anything to do with it.'[73]

There were other indications, too, that the co-operation had not lasted long. The National Right to Work Council was certainly not supporting its London Committee financially. It had no difficulty at all in raising the £250 necessary to finance a national conference which it held early in December 1908, and yet in January the Joint London Committee was appealing for money, Quelch claiming that Greenwood was apparently expected to 'live on air, and grow fat by expanding his lungs by open air speaking'.[74] In the middle of January 1909 Jack Williams appeared in the backruptcy court, while in November, after a summer of complete lassitude, the London Committee reported that it had in hand the paltry sum of 4s 5d (22p). Again, the annual meeting which heard this sad tale was not attended by any of the MPs who had participated in the formation of the London Committee, and the new executive elected by the delegates was dominated by Social Democrats—Fairchild, Greenwood, Williams, W. Lock, Macdonald, John Scurr, Dora Montefiore, and Mrs Hicks all being returned. But the breakdown had clearly taken place long before this.

Finally, it can be noted that in March Frank Rose, a member of the National Committee's executive, claimed in the *Labour Leader* that the Labour Party had recently received a deputation from the Central (Unemployed) Body.[75] In fact, however, as was pointed out in the following week's edition, the deputation had been arranged and manned by the London and District Right to Work Council.[76] Evidently, Rose had no idea of what the London Committee was doing. It was significant that in this disclaimer the words 'joint' and 'committee' had both been dropped from the organisation's title, indicative again of the new independence of the London body.

The co-operation between the inner group of Labour Party 'activists' and the SDP thus lasted at most from late October 1908 to early February 1909, possibly not even as long. Why was it so short-lived? From Barnes' statement in the Commons on 17 February it seems that there may have been some disagreement over tactics. Certainly Hardie had shown himself very sensible of demonstrators' human needs when organising his provincial marches in 1905 and he may have been upset by the SDP's failure to provide sufficient food for the hundreds of women and children who were marched into central London in February 1909. Secondly, some tension was apparently generated by the National Council's December conference. The 'right to work' resolution ran into some difficulty, as many of the distress committee delegates claimed that this was a controversial matter which ought to have been avoided. Thus many Social Democrats, particularly Hyndman, were quite disgusted by the tame nature of the proposals put to Asquith by the conference deputation, and the party decided to hold its own conference under the auspices of the London Committee.

Neither of these reasons was of major significance, however, especially as the National Council could presumably, had it so desired, have given the London Committee the money it needed to provide adequate food for the demonstrators in February. Much more important was the reaction of trade unionists against co-operation with the SDP. Trade union suspicion was implicit in the refusal of the TUC to send delegates to the December conference, and this was certainly not because it felt that the government's proposals had rendered such a meeting irrelevant. Indeed, it had decided to contact the Joint Board with a view to organising a separate conference itself. There were also signs of reaction among provincial trade unionists. Early in the new year the Nottingham Right to Work Committee was suddenly dissolved. Similarly, the Newcastle Trades Council withdrew its representative from its local committee, while in Manchester the trades council left the existing committee and set up a new one, entirely under its own control.

Labour Party members, even 'activists', also disapproved. Clynes disliked the violent tactics which the Social Democrat agitators frequently employed and generally encouraged, telling a group of Manchester unemployed on one occasion that he did not look for a solution in men marching or congregating in town centres but rather in the 'men who were marching intelligently to the ballot box'.[77] MacDonald and Snowden, too, had always been suspicious of the SDP, and they both asserted vehemently that they would have nothing to do with anything organised by that party when they were invited to attend the Joint London Committee's conference in February.[78] As secretary MacDonald in particular had borne the brunt of most of the attacks made on the Labour Party and had frequently been stung into vindictiveness. He told the Oldham Branch of the SDP that he had not been in the least bit surprised to receive its letter applauding Grayson's exit from the House of Commons, 'knowing as I do the general stupidity of the S.D.P. and its incapacity to understand the meaning of any political demonstration'.[79]

Hardie must have known that to work with the Social Democrats would rouse the antagonism of substantial sections of the labour alliance, and yet in October 1908 he had been prepared to take this risk for the sake of the unemployed. What had caused him to change his mind was the fact that Grayson had become the focus of the Labour Party's critics. Resolutions applauding his stand in the Commons and comparing it favourably with the Labour Party's own supine attitude flooded into the *Labour Leader* offices. 'Activists' such as Curran and Snowden were shouted down, respectively at Bradford and Liverpool, when they tried to defend the Labour Party's unemployment policy, and others of the group resorted to attacking Grayson in the press. MacDonald claimed that his supporters showed a lack of understanding of how parliamentary business was conducted.[80] George Roberts said it was sad to see 'purposeless shouting appraised as of greater value than solid insistent work'.[81] By the Christmas of 1908 it was widely rumoured that Grayson, backed by his SDP supporters and

Blatchford's *Clarion* movement, intended to launch a strong attack on the Labour Party executive at the annual conference in January. As it happened, the expected attack never materialised, for Grayson was absent from the vital session of the Portsmouth conference, claiming that he had been kidnapped by two army officers who had driven him into the country and dumped him. But the threat of dissension was real enough, and even though Hardie and some of the other 'activists' had been so frustrated by the Labour Party's failure to press home the unemployed question in 1908 that they were willing to work openly with the more militant Social Democrats, they were certainly not prepared to see their life's work, the creation of an independent working-class political party, destroyed.

Faced with this danger of schism, they decided to close the ranks of the labour alliance and to abandon both the co-operation with the SDP and the formal 'right to work' movement. This explains why the National Right to Work Council disappeared in 1909, and also why in March 1909 O'Grady, certainly one of the most vigorous of the 'activists', was to be found defending the Labour Party against its critics, arguing that it was following the energetic unemployment policy which they were demanding.[82] Any lingering desire to maintain the alliance must finally have been dispelled at the ILP's Easter conference, when the party's 'big four', Hardie, MacDonald, Glasier, and Snowden, resigned from the National Administrative Council in protest against the continuing divisive tactics of Grayson and his supporters.

CHAPTER 5

The decline of the 'right to work', 1909

EVEN THOUGH HARDIE and his colleagues had thus decided to abandon the formal 'right to work' movement sometime between December 1908 and February 1909, the 'activists' did not drop the principle of the 'right to work' or the cause of the unemployed. Despite a small drop in the number out of work in January, unemployment was still rife, particularly in the North East, the Midlands, and parts of Yorkshire, and hunger marchers from these regions were much in evidence. A party from Leeds arrived in Stroud on 3 January and several of the marchers were promptly arrested for provoking a brawl in a public house. Stewart Grey reached South Wales on 7 January and one of his lieutenants, named Williams, attempted to emulate the exploits of the 1906 land grabbers by settling on a piece of land near Cardiff. He was arrested for obstruction. Thus the 'activists' made every effort to keep the matter alive in public speeches, although their efforts were hampered partly by their parliamentary duties, partly by the need to concern themselves with those topics which were claiming public interest. Unemployment had been widely discussed since the autumn of 1908, but even though the Social Democrats organised their demonstrations to coincide with the state opening of Parliament in February, the subject was beginning to lose its news appeal as the numbers out of work decreased, and press and public alike found new topics of interest. A party with serious political pretensions could hardly ignore the great German naval scare which reached almost panic proportions in England in March, or the controversial Lloyd

H

George Budget of April and the constitutional issues to which it gave rise.

Inside Parliament, too, the 'activists' pursued the unemployment question as vigorously as possible. It was they who led the attack on the King's Speech which, failing to mention any measure except labour exchanges, also annoyed many of the trade union members who had expected something more as a result of the government's October promises. During this debate Hardie warned in a spirited speech that 'we shall not accept the present position without such a campaign as . . . will make the Government sorry for its great betrayal', and certainly during the next few months the 'activists' continued to harry the government.[1] At the beginning of March, for example, Clynes and MacDonald attacked Burns' administration of the Unemployed Workmen's Act. A week later Clynes, Barnes, Summerbell, and Hardie all supported Wardle's resolution calling for a reduction of £100,000 in the sum granted to the Local Government Board for expenses incurred in operating the Act. Although no vote was taken, the Labour speakers made it clear that the reduction had only been moved in order to facilitate a further attack on government policy. During the Easter adjournment debate Barnes headed yet another onslaught, twitting the government with its failure to produce the promised amendment of the 1905 legislation. As late as November, by which time the unemployed index had fallen to 6.5 per cent, Barnes, Hardie, and Seddon took advantage of Asquith's motion for the temporary adjournment of the Commons until the 23rd of that month to raise the unemployment question again.

All these gestures, however, were futile because, although the party usually followed the 'activist' lead, the various resolutions and amendments were rarely pressed to a vote. On one occasion Burns withstood one of these parliamentary outbursts so easily, he told Masterman, that at the end of the debate the Labour MPs had 'cooed like doves feeding out of my 'and'.[2]

This, combined with the inability of the 'activists' to stress the subject very much outside Parliament, confirmed many in their belief that the Labour Party had really lost interest in the unemployed and become totally apathetic. Thus outside pressure on the Labour MPs continued to grow. 'The whole party,' claimed an editorial in the SDP monthly, *Social Democrat*, 'has gone to sleep again.'[3]

At the end of March the London Right to Work Council distributed a circular to all labour organisations asking them to put pressure on the Labour members to move the adjournment of the House of Commons in order to discuss unemployment. It was later claimed that over 500 such resolutions were sent into Labour Party headquarters, and certainly both O'Grady and Parker were moved to write articles defending the party's existing policy.[4] Parker pointed out that an adjournment would provide at the most a little over three hours' discussion time, and that the Speaker now would not consider the matter of sufficient urgency to warrant an adjournment.[5] But the critics' hands were undoubtedly strengthened by the debate on the second reading of the Right to Work Bill which took place on 30 April.

The leading Labour speakers were John Hodge and John Ward, the latter not even a Labour Party member although it seems likely that he was put up simply to offset the criticism, freely made in 1908, that trade unionists did not want the measure. Despite the fact that Ward was a GFTU representative on the Joint Board, he had so misunderstood the nature of some changes made in the Bill over Christmas that he had to be openly corrected by Shackleton. This probably helped to produce the verdict of one paper which said that the entire proceedings had been 'lethargic and disappointing'.[6] Several other papers claimed that the Labour speakers had made no attempt to justify the principles underlying the Bill, but had merely used the opportunity to plead with the government for some action.[7] One Labour MP said later in a significant phrase that the Bill would pass 'once labour wakes up'.[8]

The lack of enthusiasm which characterised this debate may well be explained by the fact that it had been completely over-shadowed by the extremely radical and controversial Lloyd George budget introduced the previous day. George Roberts even claimed that the budget speech had been so timed pre-cisely to influence all those who had intended to vote for the Unemployed Bill.[9] There was possibly some truth in this, as the government could not have been unmindful of the embar-rassment it had suffered in 1908 through its failure to produce any realistic counter-proposals. But by this time the govern-ment had in fact got some positive measures of its own and it seems more likely that the lethargy was due to the fact that by 1909 the energies of the labour alliance, channelled for the past two years into the struggle for the Right to Work Bill, had begun to diversify.

For two years the Bill had been the only concrete legislative proposal before the country and its popularity and publicity had depended entirely on the propaganda activities of the labour movement's rank and file. At the ILP's 1909 Easter conference the executive appealed again to branch members to remember 'the great necessity of keeping the Unemployed agitation vigorously active ... the success of Parliamentary effort will depend upon the strength of the demand outside'.[10] But now in many cases these energies were being taken up with the new schemes and proposals which were appearing in 1909. Many had seen the original introduction of the Right to Work Bill simply as a sort of goad to provoke the government into producing a positive unemployment policy. The *Clarion* had claimed, for example, that the Bill's purpose had been merely to expose the reality and magnitude of the problem.[11] Shackleton had also implied this by stating that the Bill would achieve much if it secured a thorough airing of the subject in the House of Commons.[12] Now at last other suggestions were appearing: proposals designed to show how work could be pro-

vided, thus posing an obvious challenge to the Labour Party
Bill, which had really done little more than state a principle
and outline machinery by which it might be achieved. It had
done little, as Herbert Samuel had pointed out, to suggest
where the guaranteed work was actually to come from. 'The
Right to Work Bill,' he claimed, 'was nothing more than a
peroration put into the language of a statute' and they might
just as well introduce a 'right to be happy bill' whereby all
had the right to be happy and the local authorities had to
provide the wherewithal.[13] Once proposals for providing work
appeared, little was left of the Right to Work Bill except its
principle, and it became very much of an ideal or shibboleth,
rather than a statement of practical policy. In this context it is
worth noting that shortly after the second reading debate an
article in the *Socialist Review* (the monthly produced by the
ILP) admitted that it would perhaps 'never pass. It is a manifesto.'[14]

Similarly, the time and energy which the labour movement
had devoted to propagating its own ideas were increasingly
absorbed by these new programmes. This process began in a
tentative way when the royal commission appointed to investigate coast erosion reported in January. Established in 1906,
its terms of reference had been expanded in March 1908,
largely as a result of Labour Party pressure, to investigate
whether it was desirable to make experiments in afforestation
as a means of increasing employment at times when the labour
market was depressed. The report stated that if the 9,000,000
acres of suitable land were wooded, temporary employment
would be provided for 18,000 men in winter and permanent
work could ultimately be available for 90,000. Furthermore,
there were 'sufficient unemployed persons willing . . . and able
. . . who could advantageously be employed without a period
of special training'.[15] Labour men received these suggestions
very favourably because afforestation schemes had frequently
been advocated as a way of absorbing the unemployed, and

Hardie, appearing before the commission on behalf of the Labour Party, had argued strongly in favour of such a remedy, as had Lansbury who also testified.

Not surprisingly, there was a great deal of anger when no place was found for the commission's proposals in the government programme. Henderson grimly reminded Burns that on at least one occasion he had virtually promised to implement the report once it was available.[16] Hardie claimed that he had expected at least £1,000,000 to be set aside for afforestation in 1909, while Snowden told an East London audience that the matter was really 'rotten ripe'.[17] Tom Summerbell, who, along with John Ward, had served on the commission, spent much of his time in 1909 trying to popularise the report's recommendations, and the ILP published a pamphlet which he prepared for this purpose. By the end of February 6,500 copies had been sold.[18] So favourable was the labour reaction to the report that sections of the Conservative press predicted its incorporation into the Right to Work Bill. But there was no time to do this before the second reading debate came on, and after Lloyd George had presented his budget it was widely believed that the Development Bill, to which he then referred, would include some of the afforestation recommendations.

This Development Bill was designed to confer on the government the powers necessary to embark upon schemes of road improvement, marshland reclamation, afforestation, and agricultural experiment, partly to improve facilities in these spheres but also to provide useful work for the unemployed. It was this aspect of the measure which commended it to Hardie, who saw it as the means of giving work to those in need and not covered by another proposed government measure—unemployment insurance. He further argued that, in creating a central authority to frame schemes of work in advance, the Bill had lifted the main idea behind the Right to Work Bill. The Development Bill and the insurance proposals together went, he said, 'a long way towards meeting our demand for work or maintenance, as set forth in our own Bill'.[19] Barnes and Roberts supported the measure because they saw it as an attempt to substitute collective enterprise for private profit-mongering, and when it passed through the Commons in the autumn Barnes welcomed it as 'a contribution to the solution of unemployment . . . the first real attempt to deal with unemployment on the lines of what might be called organic change'.[20] Thus the Development Bill provided some challenge to the Right to Work Bill, partly by adopting some of its ideas, partly by pre-empting the need for any other measure. In moving an unemployment amendment on the King's Speech in 1911 O'Grady confessed that the Act contained all labour's proposals of the past twenty years, and although it failed to realise many of labour's hopes the *Labour Leader* could still deem it 'the most Socialistic measure on the statute book'.[21]

The insurance schemes to which Hardie had referred also began to absorb labour's attention in the course of the year, and again the claim was made, for example by the Labour Party executive report to conference, that the proposed state contributions would be the equivalent of the party's own demand for state maintenance.[22] In February 1909 the GFTU set up a small committee to gather information about all existing unemployment insurance schemes in order to submit a report to the Joint Board. There was apparently some lack of liaison here, however, for when the matter was raised the Joint Board secretary informed the federation that the TUC had already made plans to discuss the question at a special conference to be held in March. Other trade union leaders spent some time compiling a detailed list of their criticisms of a draft system which Beveridge had prepared and submitted to the TUC for comment.[23]

Perhaps the most potent source of alternative unemployment remedies came, however, in the long-awaited report of the poor law commission issued on 17 February. Although the majority report received what Beatrice Webb called a 'magnificent reception', it was not popular with working-class organisations.[24] It was the minority report, signed by Mrs Webb, Lansbury, Chandler, and Russell Wakefield, that captured their imaginations. To tackle unemployment these four recommended that a national system of labour exchanges should be set up and a ministry of labour created to replace the poor law authorities and the distress committees and be responsible for organising the national labour market. In addition, they suggested that trade unions should receive subsidies from the government for their unemployment funds, that the hours of work for all transport workers and those aged under eighteen should be reduced, and that the government should plan its own public works, which were to include afforestation and foreshore reclamation, over a ten-year period, in order to offset fluctuations in the market demand for labour. This set of very practical recommendations was welcomed by almost every working-class group. Mrs Webb had informed leading Labour MPs of the schemes as early as January 1908 and had been pleasantly surprised by their response—'almost a promise of active support'.[25] MacDonald claimed at the ILP conference that the minority report was nothing more than 'our old proposals paraphrased, brought up to date as to facts and experience, and issued at public expense'—in a sense he was right.[26] Proposals for the creation of a labour ministry and for the reduction of hours had long figured in labour programmes. But now these ideas had been blessed as part of a very full attack on unemployment by a government-appointed inquiry, and they were to be popularised by a vigorous campaign under the talented direction of the Webbs. Only the Social Democrats were hostile, and it is significant that one reason for their opposition was the omission of any reference to the 'right to work'.[27]

Trade unionists welcomed in particular the idea that union unemployment funds should receive a government subsidy, and this was put very strongly to Asquith and Lloyd George by a TUC deputation at the end of February. It was pointed out that between 1897 and 1906 the hundred principal unions had spent some £4,000,000 on unemployment relief. By aiding the distress committees, it was argued, the government was indirectly helping the non-unionists and in fairness ought to provide some similar assistance to the unions. In his reply, however, Asquith immediately put his finger on a difficulty, saying that as the unions made no practical distinction between their benefit and industrial funds there would be no safeguard against their using public funds, given as an unemployment subsidy, in order to finance industrial actions. Unless the two funds were separated, he went on, there was no possibility of such a grant being made, and he further suggested that union reluctance to make such a distinction probably explained why the matter had not been raised before.[28] It is a good illustration of the way in which the government succeeded in taking the initiative away from the labour movement during 1909 that a grants-in-aid resolution was defeated at the TUC's September assembly, despite a plea from Charles Bowerman, Labour member for Deptford, that this would reflect unfavourably on the parliamentary committee in view of its earlier deputation to the government. Much of the opposition was based on the same objections, which had been raised unsuccessfully against a similar resolution moved in 1908, but several delegates in 1909 followed the lead of J. Hill of the boilermakers and argued against such grants because they were essentially a sectional solution, unwarranted when the government itself was at last considering working along national lines.

Undoubtedly, however, the greatest appeal of the minority report was to a substantial section of the ILP. Their loss of enthusiasm for the Right to Work Bill was evident when a party demonstration in London to back its second reading had to be abandoned for want of support. Between March and mid-July 1909 the ILP sold 77,850 pamphlets, of which only

800 dealt with the Right to Work Bill and a further 500 with the more general aspects of the unemployment problem.[29] Together, this represents a total of just over 1.6 per cent of the total sold in this period, compared with 20,500 unemployment pamphlets sold out of a total of 141,000 between March 1908 and 20 February 1909, or 15 per cent of the total.[30] Clearly unemployment bulked less large in the party's propaganda activities in 1909.

Much of the impetus behind the ILP's support for the minority report came from the party's national executive, which informed one inquirer in September 1909 that the party was backing the Webbs' National Committee to Promote the Break-Up of the Poor Law established in May. The object of this organisation was explicit in its title and the support given by the ILP's national executive reflected the views of some of the new members elected at the annual conference. One of them, J. M. McLachlan, had advocated as early as 1908 that the Labour Party should abandon the policy of modest palliatives and concentrate on a national campaign ranging over the whole spectrum of poverty.[31] This was just what the minority report offered, and in this way it was a challenge to the almost exclusive support which the Right to Work Bill, essentially a single solution to a single problem, had enjoyed from ILP members.

Sidney Webb was very keen to bring the unemployment proposals into prominence, for even before the reports were issued he was making arrangements with the ILP to hold a major demonstration to publicise them. When this meeting eventually took place, Webb, perhaps unwittingly, criticised the Right to Work Bill. Unemployment, he claimed, would not be solved in one session of Parliament. 'The solution is not to be found in one word, such as Socialism with a big "S" or in two words, such as Tariff Reform. There is no one panacea.'[32] At the ILP's annual conference a delegate from Norwich advocated that they should now strive for unemployment legislation on the lines of the minority report, which he described as 'the last word'. More significantly, he went on to criticise the Right to Work Bill on the grounds that it was not a national solution because local committees were to be created and some of the necessary monies were to be raised from local sources.[33] It was perhaps symbolic of the challenge presented to the Right to Work Bill by the minority report that George Lansbury, formerly an executive member of the National Right to Work Council, became a vice-president of the Webbs' committee in 1909.

The ILP was not alone in withdrawing much of its energy and time from the campaign for the Labour Party's own Unemployment Bill in 1909. As we have seen, there were several who felt that the government had conceded the 'right to work' demand in the Development Bill and the proposed unemployment insurance. A similar view was apparent when, in May, Churchill introduced his labour exchange system. Thus Clynes claimed that it was really a part of the Right to Work Bill.[34] The same implication was behind Henderson's remark that the government had begun to take the measure out in penny numbers.[35] Equally significant in diverting attention from the Bill itself was the amount of time devoted, particularly by the trade union movement, to the actual details of the new scheme.

Exchanges, of course, were nothing new, dating back in London to the 1880s. In 1906 Beveridge, the architect of the present scheme, had pursuaded the Central (Unemployed) Body to set up a system in the capital under the provisions of the Unemployed Workmen's Act. He had even then been aware of the need for trade union support and had done his best to meet the very stringent conditions the London unionists had demanded in return for their blessing. The TUC had been concerning itself with exchanges for some time before the new national programme was brought forward, sending a four-man team to Germany in 1908 to examine at first hand the working of the German system. Once the introduction of a national scheme in Britain was announced, the TUC spent a good deal of time and energy mobilising and organising union opinion. A meeting of 220 delegates, representing 1,550,000 workers, was held in March 1909 in order to discuss both exchanges and insurance, and a constant stream of trade union deputations carried opinions, fears and reservations to the Board of Trade.

So thoroughly did the TUC concentrate on the exchanges that it frequently failed to let the Labour Party know what was being done and in July this produced a heated exchange at a Joint Board meeting. In opening the meeting Shackleton said that Churchill by now was well aware of trade unionists' views, which brought an immediate protest from Henderson and the other Labour Party representatives on the board because, it was claimed, the trade union deputations had acted before any common policy had been agreed upon. Henderson added that he had been forced to deal with many questions concerning the exchanges, often unaware of the attitudes adopted by the various deputies, and constantly 'hampered by the fear that contradictory suggestions might have been advanced'.[36] He further complained that many amendments had been put down of which he had known nothing, although he had been expected to discuss them. (In the light of this complaint it is worth noting that during the committee stage of the Labour Exchanges Bill, Beveridge told his mother of one Labour MP who had put down a whole series of amendments, but because he had acted without first consulting his colleagues he was 'made to stay away when he ought to have moved his amendments and they fell to the ground'.[37]) But the members of the parliamentary committee were not slow to defend their actions. W. J. Davis pointed out that the Labour Party could easily have requested a Joint Board meeting had it really wanted to discuss a common policy, while both Shackleton and Bowerman said that in the past circumstances had sometimes made it necessary for the Labour Party to act without first consulting the other members of the board and the plea of exigency had always been accepted. After some discussion Henderson moved that the board should investigate how far separate action by any one body with regard to prospective labour legislation could be avoided. This was agreed to, despite Shackleton's assertion that he would not do this if it meant that the TUC had to consult the Labour Party every time before it acted.[38]

Although the Labour Exchanges Bill had its first formal reading on 20 May 1909, Churchill had already taken advantage of a discussion on the poor law to indicate the main lines of the scheme. The exchanges were designed, he said, to cope with two deficiencies—the immobility of labour, and the lack of information about the labour market. They would be of use in estimating the seasonal and geographical requirements of certain trades and in encouraging school-leavers to enter prosperous trades rather than dying ones. It was hoped to divide the country into about ten areas, each with a divisional clearing house and with 30-40 first class exchanges (in cities with populations of over 100,000), 45 second class (population 50-100,000), and about 150 minor offices and sub-offices. Although the whole system would be controlled by the Board of Trade there were to be in each area joint advisory committees to ensure impartiality between capital and labour. They were to consist of equal numbers of representatives of workers and management with a neutral chairman.

Labour leaders were not slow to appreciate that there were good reasons for supporting such a system, provided the questions of control and administration were satisfactorily dealt with. It was argued, for example, that the government was set on establishing the system and that to ignore it would mean that it would fall into the hands of the free labourers, a point of no little significance as the National Free Labour Association had already made representations to Churchill seeking some role in the administration.[39] Others pointed out that the exchanges were to be used for registering workers, a necessary step towards dovetailing the supply and demand for labour. Probably the most potent argument for their acceptance, however, was the fact, stressed by Churchill, that they were a necessary preliminary to any insurance plan.

Naturally there were fears and objections which had to be thrashed out. Firstly there were what can be termed the miscellaneous arguments, springing usually from particular trades or interests. Thus the seamen's leader, Havelock Wilson, was totally opposed to any form of exchange system on the grounds that the special bureaux which had been run for sailors over the past sixty years had been a complete failure, and during the second reading debate Wilson moved that the Labour Exchanges Bill be deferred for six months. James Sexton, leader of the Liverpool dockers, was afraid that registration and classification would put some men permanently out of work. In Liverpool, he argued, there were 22,000 dockers of whom 15,000 were in work at any one time. If dock labour was decasualised and registered the unlucky 7,000 would always be the same men.[40] The general labour unions were also disturbed by the prospect of classification, fearing that unskilled men would suffer, and they demanded that their position *vis à vis* the skilled men should be guaranteed.[41]

There were also fears that union wage rates and conditions would not be observed by the exchanges, Curran arguing strongly during the second reading debate that no job should be offered at less than union rates and conditions. Against this, however, other union leaders said that to insist on such a concession would cause the whole scheme to break down, and at the end of July the Joint Board decided to press Churchill for a regulation simply compelling employers to state clearly what they were prepared to pay for a particular job. This he agreed to do, pointing out that it would be extremely difficult to enforce any suggestion for union rates.

Most fundamental of all, however, was the feeling that exchanges were potentially dangerous because they could be used
as recruiting agencies during times of industrial dispute, and
Curran claimed at the special March conference that all existing bureaux had been used for this purpose. But here the
value of the earlier TUC investigation into German exchanges
became apparent, for Bowerman was able to point out that
this had been one of the main fears held by German unionists,
but experience had shown it to be groundless.[42] In any case, as
Wilkie later pointed out, if an employer was intent on recruiting blacklegs it was obvious that he would be more successful
—and more anonymous—on the back streets of a town than in
the exchange, where the moral pressure exerted by the pre-
sence of trade unionists would probably be sufficient to deter
most potential blacklegs.[43] Despite this, Henderson argued at a
later Joint Board meeting in favour of throwing the exchanges
out of gear when a dispute was taking place and he was supported by Tillett. O'Grady said that really there was little to
fear if information were carefully presented, perhaps by post-
ing notices on the exchange walls about any dispute, and
Richards added that if the exchanges did supply blacklegs
then a trade union boycott would soon cause them to collapse.
Bowerman clinched the argument as far as the Joint Board
was concerned by saying that originally German exchanges
had been closed during disputes and it had proved a complete
waste of time.[44] Although Henderson was thus outvoted at this
meeting of the Joint Board, his suggestion was raised again at
the TUC conference in September, but it was defeated.

These reservations about the exchanges explain why labour
took so much interest in the question of their control and
management. Much depended on the quality of the administrators and their impartiality. Clynes claimed that the workers
would only accept the exchanges if they were given equal representation on the advisory committees, while Joseph Pointer,
a Labour by-election victor making his maiden speech, affirmed

that the men would be extremely suspicious if they had no representation.[45] Particularly sensitive on this point were the general labour unions, who were naturally the most subject to exploitation, and also the men in the engineering and ship-building industries who had suffered in the past from the blackleg activities of the free exchange run by the Shipbuild-ing and Engineering Employers' Federation. In fact, there was little to fear, for Churchill had told Asquith as early as Janu-ary that equal representation for workers and management was to be the root principle of trade boards, labour exchanges, and insurance committees. But the slowness of the Board of Trade in appointing the administrative bodies certainly in-creased the workers' suspicions. They had still not been set up by the time the first exchanges opened in January 1910.

Springing directly from this concern with control came labour's interest in the quality of the men appointed to the managerial posts. Some were afraid that civil servants were being offered special incentives to apply, and after consider-able pressure had been put on him in the Commons Churchill announced in September 1909 that all local officers would be selected by three-man committees, representing labour and capital, chaired by a neutral civil servant. The chief appoint-ments, however, he intended to make himself, and he tried to offset any hostility which this might have created by appoint-ing Shackleton to advise him on such positions. It was prob-ably no surprise to trade union leaders when Beveridge was given the post of Director of Exchanges, but the large number of other public school men who got appointments caused alarm in trade union circles and early in 1910 the GFTU set about preparing a report on the social backgrounds of the labour exchanges' administrators.

Undoubtedly, a good deal of the labour movement's caution about the system evaporated when it was seen to be geared into a larger scheme of relief dependent on the financial pro-visions of the budget. Thus long before the budget was presented Hardie dismissed exchanges on their own as 'an insolent attempt to fool the nation'.[46] Barnes adopted a culinary metaphor and damned them as 'mustard without the beef'.[47] He changed his mind, however, when the details of Lloyd George's budget were announced because it was partly designed to pro-

MISS BUDGET : "Is that man a friend of yours ? "
LABOUR PARTY : "Oh, he's a poor out-of-work who wants me to help him, but I'll see you home first."
THE UNEMPLOYED : "He seems to have forgotten me since he's taken up with that hussy."

Justice, 6 Nov 1909

J

vide money to link up the exchanges to schemes of development, afforestation and insurance. This must help to explain
the strong support which the labour movement gave to this
Finance Bill. 'Socialists,' wrote Snowden, 'may regard the des-
tination of the new taxation with every satisfaction.' [48] There
were other reasons behind labour's support, of course. Even
more of the revenue was intended for the old age pension
scheme introduced the previous year. The principles behind
the new taxes were highly acceptable as they represented an
attack on landed monopoly, and many of the new or increased
charges had been advocated by a Labour Party conference on
taxation at the beginning of the year. Finally, there was again
the simple political consideration that to have ignored such an
advanced budget would have forfeited the Labour Party's
claim to be a serious radical contender for political power.

But whatever its causes, the interest of the labour alliance
in the budget again served to intensify the processes by which
the amount of time and activity devoted to the Right to Work
Bill was sapped. In November *Justice* printed the cartoon
reproduced on the previous page. Strictly speaking, this charge
was unfair, as support for the budget was not entirely irrelevant to the unemployment question, and most sections of the
labour movement were still anxious to see the problem tackled.
The difference was simply that now the movement's energies
were going into other people's ideas rather than into its own
Right to Work Bill. By the second half of 1909, neither the
Bill nor the ideal occupied the elevated status that they had
enjoyed in the movement's unemployment policy for the previous three years.

CHAPTER 6

A wasted year, 1910

THE PREVIOUS CHAPTER traced the beginnings of the process by which the enthusiasm and time that the labour movement gave to the principles embodied in the Right to Work Bill were side-tracked in 1909 by the appearance of several more practical proposals for relieving unemployment. Naturally such a shift of emphasis did not take place overnight and the fluid state of opinion is well illustrated in the Labour manifestos issued during the general election of January 1910. This contest was brought about by the refusal of the House of Lords to pass the Lloyd George budget and unemployment consequently played a very minor role beside the budget question and the constitutional issues to which the peers' action had given rise. But twenty-two Labour candidates stated that the government's own legislation had made, or would make, a significant contribution towards solving the problem, while others, including MacDonald and Roberts, added that this programme had realised a substantial part of the Right to Work Bill.

The proposals of the minority report were also much in evidence, the eleven candidates who referred to them including Barnes, soon to be made party chairman, Henderson, whom he replaced, and W. C. Anderson of the ILP executive. Six of the eleven also mentioned the 'right to work'.[1] The manifesto put out by the ILP gave almost equal prominence to the two approaches. Both J. H. Belcher, another member of the executive, and George Barnes wrote in the *Socialist Review* that the way to tackle unemployment was through the Right

to Work Bill *and* the suggestions contained in the Minority
Report.[2] Shortly after the election a certain J. Edwards expressed the hope that the Bill would be amended to include
the poor law proposals.[3] A similar view was manifest in the
nine unemployment resolutions submitted to the Labour
Party's January conference. Five mentioned the Right to Work
Bill, two in conjunction with the minority report. Three of
six resolutions dealing with the poor law were framed with
reference to the unemployment problem.

There were still those, of course, to whom the 'right to work'
principle was of more importance than any of the alternative
schemes, and they were highly critical of the party's failure to
stress it during the election campaign. One delegate to the
annual conference, for example, argued that the budget should
have been condemned and an all-out stand made on the Right
to Work Bill. Another party member wrote to the *Labour
Leader* regretting that 'unemployment and the right to work
. . . were not the central issue of the Labour campaign during
the election'.[4] In the *Clarion* Blatchford used the same line of
argument to keep up his almost continuous indictment of the
Labour Party. 'The deserters,' he thundered, had been 'so
busy defending free trade against the assaults of the Tariff
Reformers that (to them) such insignificant problems as unemployment and poverty appear to have been forgotten.'[5]
When the election left a forty-strong Labour Party and just
over eighty Irish Nationalists holding the balance between a
severely weakened government and an opposition almost equal
in size, many labour stalwarts anticipated that this favourable
position would be used to force through the Right to Work
Bill. The expectation was clearly widespread, for H. R. Maynard, who had been the first clerk of the Central (Unemployed)
Body, told Beveridge that he was afraid MacDonald might use
his party's advantageous position for 'forcing relief schemes or
rights to work upon the Board of Trade'.[6]

But the Right to Work Bill did not appear in 1910, nor was

any unemployment amendment moved on the King's Speech,
a decision which brought relief to Asquith who seems to have
shared Maynard's forebodings. Barnes, Asquith told the King,
'spoke in a more friendly tone than had been anticipated'.[7]
It was later explained that O'Grady and Thorne had decided
not to move an amendment for fear of bringing down the
government, and the priorities implied by this decision—that
O'Grady and Thorne preferred to allow the government to
get on in peace with the task of curbing the powers of the
House of Lords—were shared by many other Labour members, including some of the 'activist' group: Summerbell,
Snowden, MacDonald, and Seddon, for example. At Cardiff
Snowden said that there was no alternative to the fight with the
peers if they wanted the budget, even though such a struggle
would take time.[8] Even Barnes, one of the most ardent supporters of the unemployed, said in February that nothing
should be allowed to obscure the question of the Lords' veto,
which incurred him some criticism at the ILP conference.
MacDonald felt that the Labour Party should concentrate on
'stiffening the back of the Government so as to get the suprem-
acy of the Commons settled once for all'.[9] He was so keen on
this that in April he was urging the Liberal Chief Whip, the
Master of Elibank, to stand firm against the threats of the Irish
not to support the budget, saying that to give in would be to
strengthen the House of Lords.[10]

Only two of the 'activists' apparently disagreed with this
policy. Hardie admitted at the ILP conference that the immediate result of moving a successful amendment on the
King's Speech would have been another general election, but
it would, he said, have been fought on an exclusively labour
issue—unemployment. He had already stated at Swansea in
March that questions concerning unemployment and the 'right
to work' were the special concern of the Labour Party which
could not, therefore, allow itself to be sidetracked into prop-
ping up a tottering government.[11] His view was shared by

Jowett who feared that if the party concentrated on the constitutional question social issues like unemployment would be
lost sight of entirely.[12] Perhaps more significant from the point
of view of the party's subsequent history was the disgust of
Leonard Hall, a member of the ILP's National Administrative
Council. 'If there was a firm bargain ... something tangible,
for instance, for the scores of thousands of poor devils swarm-
ing round the doors of the Labour Exchanges, one could
understand. But there is nothing.'[13] It was no coincidence that
later in the year Hall helped to compose the famous 'green
manifesto', *Let us reform the Labour Party*, which accused the
party, among other things, of neglecting the unemployed for
the sake of political expediency.

But even if the majority of the Labour Party had agreed
with Hardie and Jowett in keeping the unemployed as the
main priority there were other very persuasive arguments
against doing anything very positive. For one thing, if the
party had managed to bring the government down it almost
certainly could not have afforded to fight another election so
soon on any large scale. The January campaign had been a big
strain and now the party's finances were threatened by the
effects of the Osborne judgement. In this action, brought by
W. V. Osborne against his union, the Amalgamated Society
of Railway Servants, the Law Lords had decided that trade
union contributions to maintain MPs were not among the
legitimate objects of unions as defined in the Trade Union
Acts of 1871 and 1875, and that they were thus *ultra vires*.
This struck at the very basis of the Labour Party's independence and made the prospect of a second election distinctly unwelcome. It had also a second effect, and this was to cause the
Labour Party and the union movement to devote most of their
independent activities during 1910 towards securing a reversal
or annulment of the judgement.

As early as 7 January the Labour Party had begun to draft a
Bill to provide for the payment of MPs, and at some time be-

tween January and April, when the 1909 budget was again
passed in the Commons, MacDonald wrote to Lloyd George
saying that unless the government introduced a Bill or resolution providing for the payment of members, or allowed time
for the Labour Party's own Bill, he would withhold party support from the budget.[14] The Liberals, in fact, talked out a
resolution on this subject, but Asquith kept Labour's hopes
high by his sympathetic reception of a deputation in the summer. As the year went on, the campaign to cancel the decision
assumed growing importance, and by August the *Labour
Leader* was terming it the 'question of questions'.[15] The party's
annual autumn campaign was devoted to a drive against war
and to the reversal of the Osborne ruling—'the one thing of
supreme and overwhelming importance'.[16] Not surprisingly,
Osborne was also the burning topic of interest at the TUC's
September conference.

Again, just what proposals were the Labour Party to bring
forward? As indicated in the previous chapter, many were
questioning the usefulness of the Right to Work Bill and seem
to have felt that it was no longer very relevant in the light of
legislation introduced or pledged since it had first been
drafted. MacDonald claimed in February that 'much of the
Bill had already been adopted by the Government . . . much
more of it, owing to the passing of the Development Act, has
been withdrawn from the sphere of legislation and placed in
that of administration'.[17] Snowden shared this view, and one
critic claimed that his acceptance of unemployment insurance
was tantamount to selling the Labour Party's birthright for a
mess of pottage. 'It is absurd for Mr Philip Snowden to assert,
as he does, that the Labour Party's Right to Work Bill is conceded in the above reform unless he holds the view that 7sh
or 8sh is a living wage.'[18] Some ardent supporters of the Bill
were so incensed by these statements that they put down a
censure motion on Snowden and MacDonald at the ILP's
annual conference and were only persuaded to withdraw it at

the last moment. In July Henderson repeated his claim that
the government was taking the Bill out in penny numbers,
this time to the General Council of the GFTU.[19] Even those
who did still feel that the principle of the measure was valuable were compelled to confess that the Bill needed re-drafting.
Hardie, for instance, admitted in June that it had been overtaken by events and said that it was necessary to make provision in it for co-ordinating the work of the labour exchanges
and development commissioners, and for providing maintenance in the form of insurance administered by a trade union.[20]

Thus, given the differing views about the desirability of
passing the Right to Work Bill, the need to revise it, and the
general sense of priorities held by most members of the parliamentary Labour Party, it was hardly surprising that the Bill
was not even on the party's programme for 1910. First place
went to the Trade Union Bill, designed to offset the Osborne
decision. In any case, unemployment was not very pressing,
being down to 5.7 per cent by February, and four months later
Hardie granted that the question had 'ceased to attract that
amount of attention it claimed during the depression'.[21] The
lack of urgency is clearly seen in the fact that it was not until
April that the Joint Board set up a sub-committee to begin the
work of re-casting the Bill, and although this task was completed by July the details were still being discussed in October.
When the second general election of 1910 took place in December only a third of the Labour candidates mentioned the
Bill at all. This compared with the 81 per cent who stressed
the Osborne case, perhaps a reflection of the party's general interests throughout the year as well as of declining enthusiasm
for the Bill.[22] Significantly, eleven of the thirteen who had
mentioned the measure in January and who now omitted it
were MPs.[23]

It is doubtful in any case whether the Bill would have received the undivided attention of the labour movement even
if it had been re-introduced in 1910. The members of the ILP

were still torn between the 'right to work' and the minority
report, and when the national council decided to devote the
annual summer campaign to propagating the report's proposals for dealing with poverty, destitution, and unemployment,
the ardent supporters of the 'right to work' ideal protested so
much that in July it was found necessary to issue a public
statement to the effect that the council had chosen what it
regarded as the best topic for the campaign, even though it was
appreciated that some would disagree with the choice. One
typical protester expressed the hope that the poor law campaign would not detract from the demand for the 'right to
work'.[24] The effort was backed by the Webbs' committee,
which had also been responsible for the earlier introduction of
the Prevention of Destitution Bill of which George Roberts
had said 'it is really the first endeavour to thoroughly analyse
the cause and effects of unemployment and to provide a solution'.[25] Little wonder that the devotees of the Right to Work
Bill were alarmed by the stress put on the minority report's
unemployment programme during the summer campaign.
When it culminated in a two-day conference in October, a
proposal that the report be implemented was only passed when
it was amended to include a clause demanding the recognition
of the 'right to work'. This conflict within the ILP between
the two programmes caused the *Clarion* to say, early in 1911,
that it was about time trade unionists and socialists made up
their minds to 'sit on one of two stools'.[26]

It seems unlikely, too, that the trade union movement would
have been inclined to spend much time on the Bill in 1910,
and Thorne in fact warned delegates at the September congress that there was little chance of its ever passing unless they
bestirred themselves. But Osborne hung like a cloud of doom
over the movement, and a further distraction was provided by
the outbreak of industrial unrest, particularly in the South
Wales coalfield where young militants showed every sign of
rebelling against the official leadership and its traditional

methods. Both the TUC and the GFTU were also keeping a very close watch on the teething troubles of the infant labour exchange system which had come into operation at the beginning of the year. These troubles were apparently quite severe. Beveridge told his mother that 'every few minutes we get telegrams . . . one simply daren't leave the machine alone any more than one would a locomotive'.[27] Stephen Tallents, who joined the Board of Trade in 1909, wrote later that 'the new service, I gathered, was having much difficulty . . . the office was falling into disorder and public disrepute'.[28]

With this situation at head office it was hardly surprising that there were mistakes at lower levels, and the Social Democrats, who had been against the exchanges right from their inception, played up every unfavourable incident in a bitter press offensive sustained throughout the year. In September, for example, *Justice* printed the following letter, which had been distributed to local employers by the manager of the Bradford exchange.

> Dear Sirs,
>
> Since the Labour Exchanges opened on February 1, 1910 there have been two disputes in the woolcombing industry and during the progress of both these unfortunate occurrences, some Employers applied to the Labour Exchange for men, and in both instances we were prepared to help them all we could. . .
>
> May I appeal . . . that I may be favoured with your orders for men, women, boys and girls, seeing that we were prepared to help your trade during troublesome times, I believe some reciprocation of our efforts may be shown. . .
>
> A. Heaton
Manager.[29]

Here, it was claimed, was ample evidence that the whole system was simply one for supplying blacklegs, but the local trades council, which took the matter up with G. R. A. Ask-with, the Board of Trade's industrial adviser, was informed that this circular had been issued without the knowledge or consent of headquarters, and Heaton was suspended pending a full inquiry. The national labour organisations also adopted a more constructive approach and the GFTU asked its member unions to report direct to federation officials any such cases of irregular conduct so that these could be sifted, investigated, and then taken to the Board of Trade. Similarly, when it was announced in July that the working of the system was to be debated in the Commons, the Labour Party executive circularised all local bodies asking if there were particular points or criticisms which might be raised.

There is little indication that the majority of trade unionists shared the dogmatic hostility of the SDP, although there was much dissatisfaction with the everyday running of the exchanges. This accounts for the apparent paradox between the massive TUC vote in favour of a resolution that they were working inimically to trade union interests and the fact that Beveridge was able to tell an international labour conference that English trade unionists had generally accepted the system's advantages.[30] Possibly, too, there was some difference of opinion between the union leaders and the rank and file members who were, after all, most affected. Most of the union secretaries encouraged their members to use the exchanges, but while many local trades councils invited exchange officials to explain the new machinery to them and seem to have been anxious to make use of it, Shackleton had to defend the parliamentary committee at the TUC conference against delegates critical of the failure to insist that the exchanges should only offer work at union conditions and rates. Again, he had to point out that it was the parliamentary committee itself which had decided that they should remain open during trade disputes, a decision which had created several practical difficulties which the committee had done its best to iron out in consultation with Buxton, the new President of the Board of Trade. The degree of rank and file discontent apparently varied from area to area. At a special conference held in the autumn to mark the fiftieth anniversary of the foundation of the London Trades Council all the London delegates attacked the exchanges, although it is not clear how far the criticism sprang from actual experience and how far from the considerable Social Democrat influence in the council. Representatives from Birmingham and Nottingham, in contrast, had few complaints.

Many of the administrative complaints could clearly have been avoided had the advisory committees been appointed earlier, and this was one of the numerous points which TUC deputations raised with Buxton in a series of meetings throughout 1910. But by January 1911 nine were in operation and another four in the process of being set up. Although criticisms of the exchanges continued to be made right up until the outbreak of war in 1914, they had become much less heated by 1911 and in February of that year one trade unionist told Buxton that suspicions now were directed solely against the administration rather than the actual system. Buxton replied that there were only two classes of complaint—those based on bad administration, which would inevitably decrease as time went on, and those founded on unsubstantiated rumour.[31] When labour exchanges were discussed at the TUC conference later in the year some delegates protested that the resolution, which dealt only with the grievances of those actually employed in the exchanges, did not go far enough. The grouping committee explained that it had only been allowed to construct a resolution from those which had been sent in. The result suggests that those which were submitted had been extremely mild.[32]

CHAPTER 7

National Insurance and beyond, 1911-1914

WHEN THE LABOUR PARTY met to draw up its programme at the beginning of the 1911 parliamentary session the Trade Union Bill still had first place. Second was the re-drafted Right to Work Bill. It had been satisfactorily revised, but none of the Labour MPs were lucky in the ballot for a day on which to bring it in and it was decided instead to move a 'right to work' amendment on the King's Speech. There was no fear this time that the Conservatives might vote with the Labour Party in order to bring down the government. All but the most partisan had accepted the electorate's verdict and they were shaken by two successive election defeats in the space of twelve months and unwilling to risk a third. The amendment was moved by two of the 'activists', Clynes and O'Grady, but it was noticeable that several of the others took no part in the debate and this was interpreted in some circles as proof that they felt the amendment to be unrealistic. MacDonald implied that it had been moved purely for tactical reasons when he stated that the debate had been useful in showing that the Labour Party was not necessarily going to be satisfied with the government's insurance plans, outlined in the King's Speech.[1] This use of the 'right to work' simply to put timely pressure on the government explains why Lansbury, who had managed to win a seat in the December election, could say in March that the party had no pledge to the idea at all.[2]

Certainly in the early part of 1911 there was a revival of interest in the eight-hour day as an unemployment solution, attributable in part to the Webbs' campaign on behalf of the minority report. This remedy, of course, had never been very far beneath the surface of labour thought, but had lost much of its early impetus since the struggles of the 1890s. By February 1911, however, Ben Turner, the textile workers' leader, could claim that the matter was once again ranking high in importance. 'We want,' he wrote, 'to regain some of the spirit of the early nineties.'[3] At the same time the ILP was making plans to devote its summer campaign to the eight-hour question.

The move away from the Right to Work Bill was further accentuated in 1911 when for the first time its economic viability was severely challenged in a long debate in the correspondence columns of the *Labour Leader*. This began in February with a letter from a writer signing himself 'Lux', who argued that the maintenance clause had only been included in the Bill because socialists realised that work could not be found under the existing system. But, he went on, if the rates were increased to provide this maintenance, spending power would be reduced and unemployment would therefore rise. Afforestation and similar projects envisaged by the Development Bill and welcomed by the labour movement would also create unemployment because they would merely divert capital from one enterprise to another.[4] This provoked seven replies in the following week's paper, some of which suggested, significantly, that the maintenance should be provided through insurance. A week later G. D. Benson of the ILP wrote to say that no one had grasped the basic point which 'Lux' was making—that the provision of maintenance would divert money from other projects and thus create fresh unemployment in other sectors. 'I am afraid,' he concluded, 'that the I.L.P. will have to overhaul some of its cherished notions and subject them to a very close scrutiny.'[5] In a later letter Benson argued that if the problem was really one about the direction of capital —as most writers seemed to agree—then the answer to unemployment did not lie in a Right to Work Bill.[6] This discussion lasted until 19 May when the editor declared it closed, forty-eight letters having been published.

None of the writers had directly mentioned the minority report and it seems that there was by now a growing feeling in the ILP that the Right to Work Bill was useless, irrespective of the minority report alternative. Others, who had never favoured the minority report, were inclining more and more to the view that the government had adopted most of the Bill's demands, particularly with the announcement of insurance. One writer, lamenting the fact that a 'whole fruitful group of ideas centring round and emanating from the Right to Work' had been 'supplanted by a barren group relating to poor law administration', went on to claim that the Bill had been merely for

> educational purposes and introduced as a kind of quarry ... from which Governments could dig solid blocks of unemployed legislation... The demand for maintenance is translated into a scheme of insurance against unemployment: the demand for work leads to development schemes... It forces the state to assume responsibilities which compel it to readjust the economic system which results in poverty. That is the value of the Right to Work claim. It belongs to those great creative agencies which result not in better administration or in any other palliative, but in fundamental economic changes which are organic and therefore permanent in their value.[7]

Thus when Hardie took advantage of the ten minute rule to bring in the Right to Work Bill on 10 May it passed barely noticed and made no progress, perhaps also overshadowed by the magnitude of the Insurance Bill introduced a few days previously by Lloyd George. The influence of the minority report was very evident in the re-drafted measure, for Hardie affirmed that the 'underlying feature of the Bill is that great undertakings of public utility and Government contracts shall be arranged in advance', and certainly it now envisaged, as the minority report had suggested, that the government should plan its works over a ten-year period.[8] It was significant that Hardie stressed this aspect, for the two main principles of the older version, 'right to work' and rate aid finance, both remained. The new draft also showed the impact of the government's own legislation, as the local unemployment committees were now to be geared to the labour exchanges and to the Board of Trade instead of the Local Government Board. The Social Democrats, who had welcomed the original Bill, were very contemptuous of the new one, Quelch claiming that it was so tame that the government could almost accept it if the 'right to work' clause were replaced by one dealing with insurance.[9]

The insurance scheme had been maturing for some time before Lloyd George introduced it on 4 May. The TUC in particular had kept in close touch with the Chancellor ever since the end of 1909 and the rank and file of the labour movement had exhibited keen interest in it. In 1910 the September congress of the TUC had passed a resolution demanding certain safeguards in any insurance system in order to protect the integrity of the unions. Although Snowden had begun to argue in the same year that the government should put up all the money for any insurance scheme, outright opposition had been limited to a few such as Lansbury and Tillett. Consultations between the government and TUC leaders continued into the new year, and after one such meeting on 9 January Asquith informed the King that it had been decided to merge the two plans for insurance against unemployment and ill-health into one Bill. It was later alleged that this decision was taken as a result of labour pressure, the union leaders feeling that unemployment insurance, on which they were especially keen, would have a better chance of passing if it were part of a larger measure. This seems quite possible in view of the fact that as long ago as July 1909 Churchill had told Runciman that it did not 'seem practicable or desirable to merge the two things'.[10] Certainly the change created many difficulties for the civil servants responsible for drafting the joint Bill, for the two schemes were at different stages of development.[11]

When Lloyd George introduced the new Bill into the House of Commons he spoke for so long on Part I, which dealt with health, that he had little time for Part II, which covered un-employment, but shortly after his parliamentary statement its details were published in a supplementary press announce-ment. The plan was to cover workers in engineering, ship-building, building and construction, with contributions of $2\frac{1}{2}$d (1p) each from the worker and his employer, the state adding 25 per cent of the total thus contributed. Employers were to be able to compound their subscriptions. Benefits were payable for 15 weeks—6s (30p) a week for building workers, 7s (35p) for engineers. There was to be no benefit for men who were sacked for misconduct or who were put out of work by a trade dispute. Nor was any benefit payable for the first week of unemploy-ment. No one was to be able to claim more than one week's benefit for every five weeks' contributions. Men were to be paid through their union which would then claim the requi-site amount from a central fund. Non-unionists were to be paid through the medium of the labour exchange.

Once a scheme of such magnitude was actually before the country it was almost inevitable that it would absorb labour's attention and divert attention away from ideas such as the 'right to work' even more. Initial labour reactions were cer-tainly favourable, although there were those such as Snowden, Hardie, and several of the miners' MPs who wished that more workers were included. This also concerned the general labour unions, whose joint council was instructed to press very strong-ly for their inclusion. Similarly, many speakers at the dockers' triennial delegate meeting were concerned that dock workers had been more or less excluded. Unknown to them, however, Buxton had argued in cabinet for their inclusion on the

K

grounds that this would promote decasualisation and make the
measure more defensible.[12] But he was overruled because of
the extra cost involved, something which was apparently causing some worry to Lloyd George, for at one time he was thinking of reducing the state's contribution under Part II to 1d
per insured man, plus the administrative expenses.[13] Thus
when the question of the Bill's scope was raised by Labour
members in Parliament it was pointed out by government
speakers that it already embraced a third of the adult male
working population, the rest either being in unions which
paid unemployment donations, or employed in trades not
prone to fluctuations in the labour market. Provision was also
made for certain other trades to opt into the plan if they
wished. In addition, it was argued that the scheme was experi-
mental and before it could be safely extended more actuarial
information had to be acquired, an argument with which
George Roberts, for one, fully concurred.[14]

Criticism was also made of the clauses concerning the quali-
fications for, and restrictions on, benefits, particularly the one
which stipulated that no benefit would be paid to those who
turned down work at a 'fair wage'. As this was not defined it
was argued, for example in a Fabian manifesto issued in June,
that trade unionists would be penalised for refusing jobs at
less than union rates. The clause which denied relief to a man
off work because of a dispute was also much attacked because
it did not specify that the man had to be directly involved.
When an SDP deputation raised this with Buxton it was informed that the clause was included to prevent the insurance
fund being depleted by industrial action so that nothing was
left for the unemployed. When the matter was discussed at a
special conference arranged by the Joint Board in June, Henderson told the delegates that the Labour Party intended to
put down a suitable amendment. This was duly moved during
the report stage by Alexander Wilkie, the member for Dundee,
who claimed that the non-payment of benefit should be con-

fined to those directly concerned in a dispute by virtue of its being between their own employer and their own trade or section. But in his reply Buxton repeated that the unemployment fund was for depressions, not strikes, and added that such an amendment would encourage industrial militancy. In any case he doubted whether it would be possible to demarcate the various trades successfully. Lansbury, Duncan, O'Grady and Clynes all spoke in favour of the amendment, the latter affirming that if it was not allowed then 'the bill will commit an act of the gravest injustice to a poor and suffering class'.[15] But it was rejected 146-69.

Yet a further source of discontent was that the proposed level of benefits was different, and this was most resented, not unnaturally, by building trade workers who were scheduled to get the lower rate. The initiative in challenging this came from the secretary of the amalgamated carpenters and joiners, William Matkin, who wrote to the various building unions urging them to press for equality, and he enclosed with his letter figures to show that over a three-year period they had paid out more in unemployment benefit than the engineering unions. The Joint Board conference also decided that it was inconsistent to have unequal benefits when the contributions were the same in both cases. In July, Buxton told representatives of the building trades federation that he would assist any amendments to this clause that were permissible within the limit of the scheme's financial provisions. When the Bill reached committee W. T. Wilson, himself a building worker, moved that payment be made at a flat rate, and Buxton accepted on behalf of the government, although he strenuously opposed an attempt to include with this amendment another to reduce from one week to three days the waiting period during which no benefit was payable. The cost involved, he said, would be so great that the benefits would have to be cut down in order to finance it.[16]

The provision made for employers to compound their con-

tributions was also unpopular. A. H. Gill said in the Commons
that it was not fair that employers could make one reduced annual payment for some men because it would render the rest
permanently liable to dismissal.[17] The labour conference also
opposed this clause, agreeing that if it were passed pressure
would be exerted to gain a similar concession for employees.
But this was not very realistic, as Buxton pointed out to a
deputation from the engineering unions. Compounding was
designed, he said, to make employers regularise employment
because they were hardly likely to sack a man for whom a
whole year's contributions had already been paid. Only employers had it in their power to regularise work in this way
and it would thus be impossible to extend the idea to the
men's contributions.[18]

Many felt that the size of the premiums should be graded
according to the level of personal income. This was particularly
apposite to general labourers who were poorly paid, and it was
thus one of the suggestions which the general labourers' council was urged to press on Buxton. Socialists, too, held this view
and the ILP executive resolved to support the principle that
no one earning less than £1 a week should make any contribution at all.[19] When the Joint Board conference discussed its
committee's proposal that employers who paid low wages
should bear a larger share of the worker's contribution, Will
Thorne moved a resolution which would have exempted
lower-paid workers from making contributions at all. This,
however, was ruled out of order by Henderson.

It was also feared that the scheme would have an adverse
effect on the whole structure of unionism, although most
labour leaders were generally prepared to accept this risk so
long as amendments were made in the Bill to safeguard the
unions. The Joint Board even suggested that the scheme might
be beneficial to the union movement on the grounds that as
there was nothing to prevent an employer making wage ad-
justments so that the whole burden fell on the workers, non-

unionists would soon realise this and be compelled to join a union in order to protect their wages. But despite this optimism Beatrice Webb voiced a genuine and widespread fear when she said of unemployment insurance that 'if it is carried through, it will lead to increased control of the employer and the wage earner by the state'.[20] W. T. Wilson thought that if employers were allowed to make deductions from wages then it would be almost impossible to persuade men to join a union, and he argued that the Bill should be dropped for a year so that this point could be fully considered.[21] Victor Grayson went much further, purporting to see behind the Bill 'a sinister capitalist purpose ... it will annihilate your power to fight your employers by strike, or any other form of open aggression'.[22] His view was shared by Hall, who warned that its main object was 'to put an end to trades unionism as a fighting or even defensive force in the nation'.[23]

Because of their dislike of the scheme's contributory nature and their fears about its effects on trade unionism, Grayson, Hall and other malcontents on the left of the labour alliance were prepared to oppose the Insurance Bill outright. Their opposition was augmented by that of the SDP and the Fabian Society. The Social Democrats argued that insurance was not the right way of approaching the problem at all, as it did nothing to reduce the numbers out of work, merely keeping the unemployed worker at subsistence level until such time as he was required again by the capitalist. They were also against the contributory principle, the parliamentary correspondent of *Justice* condemning this proposal as 'mean, petty, and ridiculous'.[24] This was also the Fabians' main objection, and they decided to undertake a vigorous campaign against the scheme, beginning by issuing a critical manifesto. Within two weeks of the Bill being introduced Sidney Webb was urging Sanders to hasten the preparation of this leaflet, expressing the hope that 'the Fabian Society is not going to be as disgracefully incompetent over the Bill as the Labour Party has been'.[25] He was referring, of course, to the general approval given to the plan by the Labour MPs, many of whom were willing to accept it provided the defects were ironed out during its passage through Parliament.

But there was at this stage no unanimity within the parliamentary Labour Party. Lansbury had been arguing since 1910 that insurance would not protect the lower-paid workers, while Snowden had similarly been contending that the government should bear the whole cost. On 24 May Lansbury wrote triumphantly to Webb, telling him that at a party meeting a resolution to abolish contributions from lower-paid workers had been moved with the result that 'we have cut the party exactly in two halves. Snowden came down absolutely on the side of a *non*-contributory scheme. There is more talk among our labour men against the bill . . . now Snowden has come down on my side it is much better.' [26] Although Lansbury did not indicate in his letter who were his other supporters at this party meeting, it can be surmised from their subsequent attitude that Hardie, O'Grady, Jowett, and Thorne were among them. The first three were all members of the ILP, which had voted at its annual conference for a non-contributory system, while Thorne had argued in an article in *Justice* that the whole cost would in practice be borne by the workers, as the state's contribution would come from taxes and the employers' from increased prices. He believed that the expenses should be met from a supertax on incomes of over £300 a year.[27] Lansbury's supporters may have included W. T. Wilson, who had already argued that the workers' burdens were too great, and also Stephen Walsh, the miner, and Joseph Pointer, both of whom voted with Snowden against the money resolution sanctioning the Bill's financial provisions on 6 July.

The official party attitude was laid down by MacDonald in a long *Labour Leader* article. He argued that they were committed to abolishing low wages, but to be continually asking the government for doles, low or non-contributory insurance schemes would simply perpetuate them. Lower-paid workers would come to regard themselves as the objects of state charity and fail to join with their fellows in order to improve their conditions.[28] This argument was promptly assailed by Snowden who condemned it as 'unadulterated, sixty year old, individualism'. If state aid to raise the standard of life was wrong and degrading, as MacDonald suggested, then logically, said Snowden, he ought also to have opposed free meals for needy school children and old age pensions. It might prove impossible to get a non-contributory Bill, Snowden added, but their principles demanded that they should at least fight for one.[29]

These differences all came out at the special conference organised by the Joint Board on 20 and 21 June. Members of the ILP tried to push through a resolution making deductions from wages illegal. MacDonald opposed this, largely on the grounds that the German trade unions, which had been the subject of several Labour Party inquiries, had found a contributory system advantageous. It was also pointed out by those who agreed with MacDonald that labour could hardly demand some say in the control of a machine which it was not prepared to help maintain. Although MacDonald carried the conference with him by 223 votes to 44, this did not deter Margaret Bondfield, Mary Macarthur, and Lansbury moving a resolution to exempt sweated workers from contributing because such people already earned too little to live on. This, too, was defeated on a card vote, 1,164-284. The following day Thorne tried to move a similar resolution, this time applying to all low-paid workers, but he was overruled by Henderson.[30] It was perfectly obvious, as one union journal pointed out, that 'in relation to the trades unions of the country . . . they have not to deal with a non-contributory scheme'.[31] Lansbury was horrified by these decisions and appealed for a nation-wide agitation against the Bill.

But, as the conference had shown, MacDonald was not short of support. According to Lansbury's letter to Webb, at least half the parliamentary party were even against the abolition of contributions from lower-paid workers and it seems certain that the same members would have been opposed to a system financed entirely by the state. By and large, the trade unionists in the party backed MacDonald, and it is significant that those who opposed him most strongly belonged to unions of lower-paid or unskilled workers—Thorne of the gasworkers and general labourers, O'Grady of the furniture workers. Although the Fabian Society had come out strongly against the Bill, one of its leading members, E. R. Pease, supported the Labour Party's official policy. There was also some support for Mac-Donald from members of the ILP executive, for in inviting Herbert Bryan of the party's London organisation to one of the Fabian protest meetings, Harry Duberry, one member of the National Administrative Council who opposed the Bill, said that the demonstration would 'upset the official element on N.A.C. but we need not consider that'.[32]

The split within the Labour Party became even more apparent when the committee stage of the Bill began and the financial resolution covering both parts was debated. It made provision for the payment by the state of two-ninths of the health benefits and one-third (more than originally announced) of the total contributions made under Part II. Snowden rose and said he understood that this would be the only opportunity they had of proposing an increase in the state contribution, and he then argued powerfully for a non-contributory system of health and unemployment insurance. He only took eight other members into the lobby with him, however, and it may be that some of these voted for a free health scheme and had no strong feelings about the unemployment proposals.[33] When the financial resolution reached report stage the following day Jowett moved to abolish all contributions, withdrawing when he had explained that this was merely his way of registering a protest.

MacDonald's acceptance of the resolution was severely at-

tacked by those who claimed that it would now be impossible
to move that the state share of the contributions be increased.
He replied by submitting a memorandum (later published) to
the Labour Party executive justifying his action. He argued
that by constitutional practice only a minister could move a
resolution imposing a charge upon the state. Lloyd George
had stated that whatever benefits were paid under Part I the
state would provide two-ninths, and would pay one-third of
the total contributions made under Part II. Thus it was still
possible to move for larger benefits and the party was 'as free
to raise our points and move our amendmnets as we were
before the Money Resolution was carried'.[34] Snowden replied
in the *Labour Leader*, claiming that this statement was a tissue
of mis-statements from beginning to end and adding that there
was no chance of raising the proportion of the state's contribution. Certainly there was no possibility now of abolishing
contributions altogether, which is probably what really infur-
iated Snowden, but he went on to point out that nobody had
known on 6 July that amendments to increase the benefits
would be accepted, for the Speaker had not announced this
until the following day. MacDonald, he concluded, was dis-
honestly sheltering himself behind an interpretation of the
money resolution which no one could have held when the
Labour Party voted.[35]

But Snowden's small support in the division lobby confirms
that very few of the Labour MPs were prepared to support a
non-contributory Bill, and were certainly not willing to jeo-
pardise the whole scheme by voting against the money resolution. Not all of the ILP were prepared to risk splitting the
Labour Party either, and it was George Barnes who conducted
much of the negotiation with the government which took place
during the summer.

MacDonald's own keenness for the measure may have several
explanations. For one thing, he was the leader of an uneasy
alliance of trade unionists and socialists, and there is little

doubt that the trade union majority wanted the Bill. Beveridge stressed to his mother in August, for instance, that the union leaders were particularly anxious to secure the unemployment scheme.[36] Secondly, MacDonald seems genuinely to have believed in a contributory system, for he had written an article some fifteen years previously arguing in favour of workers' contributions to an unemployment insurance plan. Perhaps, too, he was still hankering after office and eager to ingratiate himself with the Liberal leaders. According to one source, he had already accepted one offer of a position in a coalition government projected in 1910 which had never materialised.[37] He was still in very close touch with the Liberal ministers, however. Sir George Riddell noted in his diary that one day in July 1911 when he called at Downing Street he 'found L.G. holding a conference on the Insurance Bill in his garden. Ramsay MacDonald . . . and some Government officials were seated with him under a tree.'[38] W. A. Colegate, secretary of the Prevention of Destitution Committee which had replaced the Webbs' earlier organisation, told Mrs Webb in August that there was a strong rumour circulating that MacDonald was shortly going to get office.[39] But the most likely explanation for MacDonald's attitude was his concern about the effect of the Osborne case on the unions and the Labour Party. Before the end of the session he agreed with Elibank that his party would back the Insurance Bill if provision were made for the payment of MPs.[40] In fact, Lloyd George introduced a government resolution calling for this on 10 August.

Negotiations between the government and the Labour Party continued all through the summer months, Beveridge observing on one occasion when he had spent the day discussing unemployment insurance with the Labour Party leaders that 'they were really very reasonable and pleasant and will be helpful'.[41] But MacDonald's opponents were active as well and spent the summer attacking the Bill. At the end of July the ILP and the Fabians held a joint protest meeting, despite

THE FABIAN SOCIETY
and the London and South-Eastern Counties
Division of the
INDEPENDENT LABOUR PARTY.

A **PUBLIC MEETING**
under the auspices of the above Organisations
will be held at the
MEMORIAL HALL, FARRINGDON ST.,
on FRIDAY, JULY 28, 1911,

To **Protest Against the Insurance Bill**
now before Parliament, and to demand its
withdrawal. Chair will be taken at 8 p.m. by
WM. STEPHEN SANDERS.
Speakers:
GEORGE LANSBURY, M.P.
(Member N.A.C. of the I.L.P.),
PHILIP SNOWDEN, M.P.,
MRS. PEMBER REEVES,
HENRY HARBEN,
R. C. K. ENSOR, L.C.C.,
H. DUBERY,
(Member N.A.C. of the I.L.P.).

ADMISSION FREE. A few Reserved Seat
Tickets, 2s. 6d. and 1s., can be had on applica-
tion to the Secretary, Fabian Society, 3,
Clement's Inn, Strand, W.C.; or to J. Mylles,
I.L.P. Offices, St. Bride's House, Salisbury
Square, E.C.

Protest against the
Insurance Bill.
Clarion, 21 Jul 1911

Labour Party attempts to question whether the Fabian executive had a mandate to participate in such a meeting. One of
Mrs Webb's friends described the scene at the rally.

> Philip Snowden was led on by the enthusiasm of his audi-
> ence to say more against the Bill than he ever imagined
> he could. In fact he was horrified himself and tried to
> hedge but the applause ceased at once and he went back
> to denunciation and wound up with a dramatic appeal.
> Lansbury was great and bellowed in fine style.[42]

The Social Democrats also kept up their opposition, but did
not join formally with the Fabians or the ILP dissenters. In
July, for example, Fairchild published a pamphlet under the
auspices of the London Right to Work Council, claiming that
the scheme should be free. At the TUC conference in September SDP members, backed by some of the ILP rebels, moved
against a contributory system, but were defeated by 940,000

votes to 325,000.[43] Despite this opposition campaign, however, some of its backers, perhaps influenced by this TUC vote, realised that they were going to fail, and C. D. Sharp, who was the editor of *Crusade*, the magazine produced to support the Webbs' campaign against the poor law, wrote despondently to Beatrice Webb that the only effective thing they could now do 'would be to get at the Trade Unions'.[44]

The TUC vote must also have encouraged MacDonald. At the beginning of October he wrote to Elibank again.

> I need not reassure you that the statement I made to you about the attitude of the Party on the Insurance Bill before we separated in the summer holds good. The party came to its decision, and its decision will be carried out by the officers loyally and faithfully, in spite of what two, or at the outside three, members may do to the contrary.[45]

His resolution was further strengthened when, after a long discussion, a censure motion on him in the National Administrative Council was withdrawn. It is not clear how close the debate was or who opposed MacDonald, but there were at least four men present who probably argued against his attitude— Lansbury, Jowett, Duberry, and McLachlan. MacDonald won this particular vote probably because some of the council members—those referred to by Duberry as the official element —had always felt that a contributory scheme was acceptable. Others, such as Ben Riley, thought that as the ILP members were a minority in the parliamentary Labour Party they should abide loyally by its majority decisions.[46] Certainly the split over the Insurance Bill highlighted the problems presented by the complex structure of the Labour Party. What was to be the attitude of those in the Fabian Society and the ILP, which both opposed the measure, who also belonged—by virtue of their ILP or Fabian membership—to a Labour Party which supported it? For the forty or so ILP branches which eventually broke away in the summer to form the British

Socialist Party (BSP) in conjunction with the SDP this problem had been growing for some time, and Hall, one of the
dissenters, admitted that the Insurance Bill issue had been
'the last straw that breaks the camel's back'.[47] Others preferred
to do what they had always done: remain in the Labour Party
and press their own views against the majority view dictated
by the trade union element. Thus it was not without significance that those MPs who opposed the Insurance Bill were
the remnant of the inner core of 'activists'. Curran and Summerbell were both dead, Seddon and Richards had lost their
seats, Barnes and Roberts, along with the trade union section
and the rest of the 'activist' group, had accepted that the government programme was satisfactory. Only Hardie, Jowett,
Thorne, O'Grady, and Snowden were left, joined now by
Lansbury. With the exception of the last two, these were men
who had co-operated closely with the SDP, especially in 1908,
and it might have been in an effort to resurrect the dead alliance that H. W. Lee, secretary of the provisional BSP committee, contacted the rebels to suggest that they form themselves into a parliamentary group to act in conjunction with
the new socialist party.[48] E. C. Fairchild, who had been secretary of the Joint London Right to Work Committee, wrote to
Lansbury encouraging him to keep up the fight as long as
possible, arguing that if MacDonald prevailed it would be 'the
driving under of English Socialism'.[49]

But by the time this correspondence took place resistance to
MacDonald's line had to all intents and purposes been broken.
Three days after the National Administrative Council threw
out the censure motion MacDonald contacted Elibank to inform him of the Labour Party's intentions and to offer advice
on the conduct of the rest of the session. The whole tone of
the letter bespoke of very close co-operation, almost 'rigging'.

I strongly advise you to adopt the same methods as you
did before the summer. It will be a very hard job, but I

believe you can do it. I am sorry to say that there will be one or two men whom I cannot control, but disagreements between you and the Party as a whole on the Bill will be on very few points, and upon these we can have businesslike discussions, and then divisions. I shall also be willing always to support you on any reasonable application of the closure...[50]

He followed this by issuing a public statement saying that the Labour Party intended to support the Bill when the autumn session began. This, said the *Daily News,* dispelled the impression created by the activities of the rebels during the summer that the party was divided.[51] Ten days later the *Labour Leader* acknowledged MacDonald's victory, concluding that the dissenters would simply have to make the best of things.[52] The opposition was further undermined when the actuary appointed by the Labour Party to examine the Bill presented his report. It would, he concluded, be advantageous for trade unions to join the scheme because the administrative costs would be borne by the state, and they would save because the contributions were small compared to the benefits, which the unions would no longer have to pay. What popular discontent remained was largely among lower-paid workers, and although there was some resentment at the way in which MacDonald had acted, the general feeling according to one observer was 'steadfastly in favour of the Labour Party alliance'.[53]

The Social Democrats and the Fabians kept up their opposition, but it had by now lost much of its impetus. The Labour Party rebels still refused to toe the party line and when a reassembled Parliament agreed in October that the unemployment section should be discussed in grand committee Lansbury, supported by Jowett, Thorne, and O'Grady, objected, but unsuccessfully. During the third reading debate they made a further protest, claiming that people could not afford the contributions and that both schemes should be free. But the third reading was passed by 324 votes to 21.[54]

After a year of internal dissension and negotiation, what had the Labour Party achieved in the way of amendment? Benefits had been made uniform, contributions from young apprenticed workers had been reduced, and the scheme now covered those in the scheduled trades who were aged more than sixteen, not eighteen as originally intended. Some concessions had been granted in the clauses relating to disqualification from benefit because of involvement in trade disputes, and improvements had also been made in the clauses concerning the standard of work offered to unemployed workers. The net result of these changes was an increase in the state contribution of £100,000, twice as much, said the *Labour Leader*, as the transport workers had gained from their recent strike, and readers were invited to draw the appropriate conclusions.[55] Snowden promptly pointed out that this was misleading, as the extra money had come from a surplus on the contributions, not from any increase in the state's share of the cost.[56] The rebels then made a last defiant gesture by issuing a manifesto, signed also by Hardie who had abstained on the third reading, which explained that they had been in general sympathy with the Bill's purpose, but felt that its principles were unsound. Among the objections which they listed to Part II were the contributory basis which compelled men to pay for protection against something for which they were not responsible. They also believed that the price of the benefits was too high in terms of the contributions.[57] This, however, was the last sign of their revolt, and it was perhaps indicative of the labour movement's general acceptance of the Insurance Bill that the *Labour Leader* could state that it had given them something from which to start.[58]

There were, of course, still elements which continued to demand a free scheme, or alterations in the financial arrangements in order to exempt lower-paid workers. Thus the 1912 report of the ILP urged party members to work towards a non-contributory system. In the same year the TUC unanimously passed resolutions calling for the abolition of contributions under Part II from casual workers earning less than 10s a week, and for graduated contributions from those receiving less than £1. At the end of 1912 Ben Tillett was still encouraging the members of his union to agitate for the abolition of contributions, while Thorne successfully secured the passage at Labour Party conferences in 1913 and 1914 of resolutions demanding a universal non-contributory plan. On neither occasion, however, was there any discussion, and while the labour movement may have thus defined its ultimate objective as a free system, in practice it had to accept and work with the existing legislation. In reviewing the outlook for the parliamentary session of 1912 Ben Turner stated that 'he had not much to say about the new Insurance Act. It is now law, and our business should be to make it an Act of usefulness'.[59] The majority of Labour MPs concentrated simply on the principles and administration of the existing measure, W. T. Wilson stressing in 1913 when he moved a reduction in the civil service estimates in order to initiate a discussion on unemployment insurance that 'he was not opposed to Part II of the Act' and that his criticisms would be 'concerned only with its administration'.[60]

Certainly there were plenty of administrative points which required settling. What, for example, was to happen to men who were laid off work because of bad weather? Did they receive their benefit or not? Snowden wanted to know.[61] J. V. Wills, a delegate from the bricklayers, told the 1912 TUC conference that the Umpire, appointed to arbitrate on tricky points, had decreed that in the building trade some men were covered by the Act if working in one type of job, but not in others, which meant that in the course of a single year one man could be in and out of the scheme several times.[62] Another administrative difficulty, pointed out by a TUC deputation to the Board of Trade in 1913, arose from the fact that the authorities often failed to send details of the names of union branches and members on whose behalf benefit cheques were being forwarded. Eventually, in 1914, the government did produce an amending Bill to iron out some of these problems.

The problems of dovetailing the unions' own unemployment relief systems with the state plan also took up a great amount of labour time and energy. A substantial amount of hard work was involved and at least one union secretary expressed relief that his members had decided not to opt into the unemployment scheme, because he was already overworked by the health insurance system.[63] This burden was made even greater by the fact that those unions covered by insurance were generally those which benefited most from the great increase in membership which took place after 1911. In the Operative Bricklayers' Society, for instance, membership went up in 1912 for the first time in many years—by 2,165.[64] In the same year the engineers gained over 22,000 new members.[65] It is tempting to posit some direct connection between the growth of union membership and the establishment of health and unemployment insurance, but it seems more likely that the increase was due to the prospering state of the economy and to the low level of unemployment.[66]

In turn this meant that the Labour Party's Right to Work Bill, already overshadowed by the government's programme, was pushed even further into the shade despite the high place it still occupied in the party programme. Its retention was probably due not so much to any widespread conviction of its usefulness as to the fact that adherence to the principle was one of the few remaining marks of distinction between Labourism and Liberalism. The Bill was re-introduced in 1912 and with the new title of the Prevention of Unemployment Bill in 1913 and 1914, but it was never backed by the sort of effort mounted in 1907-8 and never got beyond a first reading. The influence of the minority report was more marked than ever in the 1913-14 versions, for the Bill was now divided into two sections, the first of which made provision for the estab-

L

lishment of a labour ministry as recommended by the minority report. The 'right to work' clause only survived in the second section, no longer occupying the central place it had enjoyed in the early drafts. Resolutions in its favour were still passed at labour conferences, but the Labour Party executive resisted the few attempts made to commit it to a vigorous policy to push the measure through, and it was clear, as a delegate at the ILP's 1912 conference confessed, that it had become 'a hardy annual'.[67]

The labour movement in general was far more concerned in any case with the high level of industrial unrest which characterised the years between 1911 and 1914. 'No small part of the work . . . during the past twelve months,' reported the ILP in 1912, 'has been to aid the organised workers in their splendid industrial battles and to give legislative expression to their demands.'[68] To this end a fully comprehensive programme was drawn up by the ILP and the Fabian Society which together launched an energetic crusade against all forms of poverty in 1912. Meetings were held all over the country to popularise this programme, which was essentially that of the minority report. Unemployment was largely ignored, partly because of its low level, partly because there was really little new to say about it. But the poverty campaign must have served to strengthen the currents which were carrying the Right to Work Bill into a backwater. It was a measure designed to cope only with one aspect of poverty. The minority report and the ILP-Fabian crusade were based on a much wider concept, well expressed by W. C. Anderson at the ILP's 1913 conference.

> Social problems are not isolated and unconnected manifestations; they are interdependent; the roots of one social evil are embedded in other social evils and all find congenial soil in the poverty of the people. Problems like those of wages, hours, housing, health, child-life, unem-

ployment, pauperism, hang closely together, and so we put forward the new people's charter—a social charter this time—demanding for all the workers a standard of life compatible with the gains of civilisation.[69]

It is true that two aspects of the poverty campaign, the demand for an eight-hour day and a minimum wage, were traditional labour solutions for unemployment, but by 1912 they were both seen more as remedies for industrial unrest. Thus the speech made by Clynes at the TUC conference in 1913 advocated an eight-hour day simply on the grounds that that was as much as anybody could reasonably be expected to work in the conditions of modern industry. Similarly, a minimum wage amendment on the King's Speech in 1912 was moved not with reference to unemployment but to the 'existing industrial unrest arising from a deplorable insufficiency of wages'.[70] Unemployment, as a living political issue in Edwardian society, was dead.

CHAPTER 8

Conclusions

THE EDWARDIAN ERA saw a significant change in the attitude of the state towards its unemployed. When the twentieth century began, the worker who had no job usually had recourse to municipal relief works set up under the provisions of the re-issued Local Government Board circular of 1886, to private charity, or to the poor law. If he was a trade unionist belonging to a society that paid unemployment benefit he could, for a time, rely on that. But by 1914 the state had openly admitted its responsibility by legislating for those of its citizens who had no work. The breakthrough came in 1905 with the passage of the Unemployed Workmen's Bill, and four years later the Liberal Government began to lay the foundations of a completely new approach by setting up labour exchanges. In 1911 the National Insurance Act brought approximately one-third of all adult male workers into a state scheme of unemployment protection. It was inevitable that the increasingly articulate working classes should be deeply involved in these changes concerning a problem which affected so many of them, and unemployment thus provides a useful framework in which to study the activity and effectiveness of the Edwardian labour movement.

One can notice first the frequent initiatives taken by the Social Democrats before 1906, both in terms of general policy and direct action. It was the SDF which first interested itself in the recurring problem after the Boer War at a time when the rest of the organised labour movement was still reeling under the impact of the Taff Vale judgement. It was the SDF that first called for a special session of Parliament in the autumn of 1904, a demand subsequently taken up by other labour groups. The following year the idea of working the Unemployed Workmen's Act to death was one first advocated by the Social Democrat, Fred Knee, and soon taken up by Hardie and many of his ILP colleagues. Nor were these initiatives altogether wasted, for the SDF was quite successful in drawing attention to the unemployed, particularly in London. The street marches led by Social Democrat agitators produced considerable annoyance at many levels of society and eventually compelled the government to take steps to limit their effectiveness. This did not deter the SDF, however, and it kept the matter so effectively in the news in 1904 that by the autumn Walter Long had summoned a London conference, largely to placate the rising uneasiness which it had done so much to generate. His decision to legislate also owed much to the SDF's activity. The Liberals, too, frequently twitted in the labour press, including the Social Democrat organs, for not possessing any unemployment policy, were also compelled to give the matter some thought.

These successes were all the more surprising in view of the handicaps under which the federation worked. After November 1903 there were the regulations issued under the government's new legislation to consider, but there were other difficulties, more lasting than those posed by this restrictive measure. Numerical weakness and the uneven distribution of membership limited the scope of the agitation. Real strength was enjoyed only in London, Lancashire, and some provincial towns such as Glasgow and Northampton. Furthermore, power was heavily concentrated in London after 1901 when half of the twenty-four places on the national executive were reserved for representatives from the capital. These administrative weaknesses were well illustrated in 1905 and again in 1908 when the executive could only appeal for, rather than organise, nation-wide demonstrations. Lack of money was another perennial problem which prevented the SDF from undertaking any sustained national campaign of the type organised by the Labour Party in 1907-8. The London Central Workers' Committee collapsed in 1906 for want of funds, and had it not been for the selfless devotion of men such as Williams and Greenwood, both of whom worked on occasion for nothing, the Social Democrats would surely have made less of an impact than they did. In 1908 only the generosity of Lady Warwick made possible the fresh agitation in London, the attempt at national organisation already having failed, partly for lack of finance. But even if the federation had been organically and financially strong, its efforts in the years between 1902 and 1904 at least would still have been hampered by the various internal disputes which, rooted mainly in the question of whether or not short-term palliatives should be ignored for the sake of achieving socialism, divided the movement so deeply that in the space of just over two years it produced two off-spring—the Socialist Labour Party and the Socialist Party of Great Britain.

One other major problem which even a strong organisation would have found it hard to surmount was the frequent complacency of the unemployed themselves, although this can be exaggerated, as the exploits of the land-grabbers in 1906 and the streams of hunger marchers in 1908-9 proves. But even in London's East End, where there was a chronic unemployment problem, it was often difficult to urge the sufferers to act, and it seems more than likely that many of the unemployed only joined the demonstrations because they provided an opportunity to collect money or receive food, hence the problem posed by loafers.

Such apathy towards political and social problems was by no means unique to Edwardian Britain, but still it is strange that those who suffered from unemployment were apparently so reluctant to act on their own behalf. Obviously, unless things were really bad, as they were in 1905 and 1908, men in trade unions which paid unemployment donation had little incentive to participate in any such activity. Similarly, those with some quality or skill which in more prosperous times would usually ensure them a job were hardly likely to risk antagonising potential employers by appearing in violent demonstrations. But there remains the problem of those who had no such skill, who had almost nothing to lose, and who were out of work more often than not. They, argued Robert Tressall, were their own worst enemy who 'not only submitted quietly like so many cattle to their miserable slavery for the benefit of others, but defended it, and opposed and ridiculed any suggestion of reform'.[1] Perhaps their indifference was due to a certain mental dullness produced by months or even years of enforced idleness. W. S. Sanders was perhaps hinting at this when he said that the men who joined the socialist movement had been those who 'still retained sufficient spirit to rebel; this lifted them out of the common ruck of their class, and gave them individuality'.[2] The curious and permanent optimism noticed by Masterman might also have been important.

There was a time when things were less rosy; when we stood in knots at street corners . . . when work was solicited and solicited in vain. . . But that time seems long ago. . . We have no faith in its recurrence . . . we possess a genial faith in a Deity who is nothing if not amiable, and we are convinced that tomorrow will see the dawn of the golden age.[3]

Perhaps, too, there was an unwillingness to be exploited for political ends by an organisation with whose politics very few workers agreed, and the SDF made things worse for itself in this respect by its hostile and sectarian attitude towards trade unionists. This explains why it often tried to work through what can best be termed 'front organisations'—the London Trades Council, the Central Workers' Committee, and, later, the 'right to work' movement.

Once the unemployment question was taken up by the government at the end of 1904 it was certain that the spotlight would shift from the streets to the House of Commons. In turn this meant that the leading role which the SDF had played in organising agitation on the question passed into the hands of the other, much larger, labour organisations, the TUC, the ILP, and the body to which both were affiliated, the LRC.

The change took place really in 1905 when the LRC's activity in the House of Commons was supplemented by a national campaign of meetings more massive in scale than anything the SDF could have hoped to arrange. But initially, at any rate, the labour alliance was not free of those very problems which hampered the SDF. It did not, it is true, have the same difficulty of small numbers, as the LRC in 1903 had an affiliated membership of 847,000 trade unionists and 13,000 members of the ILP, against a recorded SDF membership in the same year of only 9,000.[4] But the TUC executive had very little real control over its constituent unions, while the ILP was not very strong in the south of England or, more particularly, in London. This may well explain the attempts made by ILP leaders in 1905 and again in 1908 to harness the London strength of the SDF in the hope that such joint action would be more effective. Nor was the labour alliance free from internal differences of the type which hit the SDF in 1902-4. There was considerable suspicion between socialists and trade unionists, well illustrated in MacDonald's efforts to conceal from the latter the ILP initiative in suggesting and financing the Unemployed Workmen's Bill demonstrations in 1905. Again, some of the ILP rank and file were very wary of their leaders' co-operation with radicals in the National Unemployed Committee, wishing the party to adopt a distinctive socialist line on the unemployed question. In the early days, too, it seems that there may have been something of a financial problem, for the demonstrations of 1905 were apparently made possible only by the timely appearance of Joseph Fels. Despite these drawbacks, however, and the total failure of the efforts to save the original Unemployed Workmen's Bill, once the LRC established a firm foothold in Parliament in 1906 the change of roles was complete and the initiative passed finally into the hands of the new Labour Party.

As a pressure group in the Commons for the unemployed the Labour Party was really, quite successful, in spite of the contentions of its left-wing critics. For one thing, the emphasis it placed on the unemployment issue almost from the day of the 1906 session contributed greatly to the eclipse of John Burns. It may be true, as tradition has it, that Burns was a proud, stubborn man in the control of his reactionary departmental officials, but he cannot have been entirely devoid of ability or Campbell-Bannerman, whose glittering cabinet testifies both to the abundance of talent available in the Liberal Party and to his own capacity for choosing able ministers, would hardly have offered him a post in 1905. Certainly the bulk of the labour movement, with the exception of his former SDF comrades, was prepared to give the new Local Government Board President every chance to show what he could do. But his refusal in the face of steady Labour Party pressure to produce any substantial unemployment policy, other than that of waiting for the poor law report, brought him into conflict with his cabinet colleagues and to the verge of resignation as early as May 1906. By early 1908 Asquith had agreed that Churchill should work out a long-term policy, and in October Labour demands for immediate action to cope with a severe depression resulted in the responsibility for a short-term policy also being taken out of his hands and placed in those of a small cabinet committee. The next two years saw the implementation of the long-term policies, and Burns faded from the scene. Small wonder that at the beginning of the 1912 session the veteran northern labour leader, Alf Mattison, could note in his diary that Burns was 'a lonely man and . . . feels his loneliness. It has been noticeable during the past session that Burns has rarely been seen and certainly not been heard in the House.'[5]

The pressure exerted by the Labour Party also succeeded in severely embarrassing the government on at least two occasions, and one Liberal minister confessed that the Labour campaign on behalf of the Right to Work Bill could well divide the Liberal left from its right. Although the actual form of the programme which the Liberals introduced in 1909-11 owed little or nothing to the Labour Party's own Bill, despite the face-saving attempts of several Labour MPs to argue otherwise, the actual fact of the programme was a tacit recognition of the success of the Labour propaganda campaign of 1907-8. It was no coincidence that the outlines of the new legislation were first discussed in government circles in the autumn of 1908, for by that time the Labour Party, aided by a somewhat for-tuitous deterioration in the labour market and a good deal of quite rowdy agitation frequently stirred up by Social Demo-crats, had suceeded in making unemployment, and more particularly the Right to Work Bill, a living political issue. As one commentator said,

> Whatever view one takes of the aims of the Labour Party, one cannot deny that they have succeeded in a way never before realised in focussing the attention of Parliament and the nation upon the . . . growing seriousness of the problem of unemployment.[6]

Considering the smallness and newness of the Labour Party these were impressive achievements. In a sense, however, it was unlucky because the great effort on behalf of the Right to Work Bill reached a climax in March 1908, six months before the worst unemployment crisis of the decade came to a head. The party had effectively shot its bolt too soon and came up against the limitations imposed by parliamentary procedure. Its attempts to keep the matter alive by outside speeches and parliamentary questions naturally appeared to be lifeless and even irrelevant as unemployment and spontaneous agitation continued to rise. The party seemed to be frittering away a golden chance to make a real and lasting impression in one of the few fields where it had a ready-made policy genuinely distinct from that of the government.

It was considerations like these which so annoyed the party's critics and which eventually produced Victor Grayson's outburst in October. Undoubtedly, as the critics maintained, there were Labour MPs who were prepared to wait for the government to produce its own answers, and who were oblivious of the wider implications of the unemployment problem because they represented only narrow, selfish trade union interests. But ever since 1906 one section of the party had put pressure on the government—MacDonald, Snowden, W. T. Wilson, Henderson, Crooks, Thorne, Jowett, Seddon, Duncan, Curran, Parker, T. F. Richards, Hardie, Barnes, O'Grady, Clynes, Roberts, and Summerbell. These were the men who launched the question campaign in 1906, made the militant speeches in 1907-8, and pestered the government front bench in 1908. It is an over-simplification to interpret their interest in unemployment as symptomatic of the division between socialist and trade unionist, if only because of the difficulty of allocating each MP neatly into one or other of these categories. In any case, not all of the group were socialists. Within this group of 'activists' was an even smaller section, consisting of Hardie, Curran, Barnes, Seddon, O'Grady, Summerbell, Roberts and Jowett, who, as well as being very vocal in Parliament, were prepared to work more or less openly with the SDF on behalf of the unemployed. Some had taken part in Social Democrat demonstrations, some sympathised with Grayson in his frustration, nearly all of whom were involved in the formation of the Joint London Right to Work Committee in October 1908.

This co-operation was short-lived, however. Several of the other 'activists' were opposed to the idea of working with the

Social Democrats, while others were afraid of the violence which generally seemed to follow them. It is possible that, initially at least, Hardie was prepared to risk their antagonism for the sake of securing something more from the government. What really caused him to forsake the alliance, apart from relatively minor disagreements, was, firstly, the reaction of trade unionists, shown in their desertion of the 'right to work' movement, and, secondly, the way in which Grayson was being used by elements hostile to the labour alliance—elements which included the SDP—to foment a rebellion against it. Hardie often expressed irritation at the cramping effects of the trade union alliance, being 'sore at seeing the fruit of our years of toil being garnered by men who were never of us, and who even now would trick us out', but in the final analysis he was not prepared to see his life's work disrupted either for the sake of the unemployed or of socialist unity.[7] He was vindicated later, for although the BSP failed in 1911 to renew co-operation with those of the 'activists' who had resisted the allurements of the government programme, kept their seats in the elections of 1910, and now opposed the Insurance Bill, it decided three years later to apply for affiliation to the Labour Party. In this way socialist unity was restored, although for a very short time, but within the context of the labour alliance.

But it seems unlikely that the co-operation of 1908 between the SDP and the inner group of 'activists' in the 'right to work' movement would have lasted very long anyway, for by the early months of 1909 the whole impetus behind the movement and the Bill was disintegrating. The Labour Party never did get its Bill through and in this sense its unemployment policy was a failure. However there were those who genuinely believed that in principle, at least, the Development Bill and the Insurance scheme conceded its basic features, while others had never really seen the Right to Work Bill as anything more than a stick with which to beat the government. For all these, the appearance of the government programme did represent the triumphant culmination of the Labour campaign.

It is possible, of course, to adopt a cynical attitude and argue that those Labour MPs who claimed that in effect the Bill had been passed only did so to hide the fact that the government had stolen their thunder. Beatrice Webb seems to have taken this view, for she noted in her diary at the end of 1910 that 'the big thing' of the past two years had been the way that 'Lloyd George and Winston Churchill have practically taken the limelight, not merely from their own colleagues, but from the Labour Party'.[8] Certainly the appearance of constructive proposals from the government benches deprived the Labour Party Bill of the support of those Liberals who had voted for it, some because they believed in it, more because they wished to protest against their leaders' failure to honour election promises. But Mrs Webb herself was partly responsible for the disintegration of support for the Right to Work Bill, because the campaign to popularise the minority report, with its comprehensive plans for tackling poverty, undoubtedly won over large sections of the ILP. It was from this same party that the first large-scale attacks on the Bill's potential came in 1911. By 1914 the Labour Party Bill bore more resemblance to the minority report than to its own antecedents, the clause guaranteeing the 'right to work' having been dethroned and given an insignificant place.

The ideal, it is true, remained as an objective—albeit a somewhat utopian one—to which the British labour movement was committed. In a way, the advent of public assistance in the inter-war period realised it, but the nobility with which Hardie and his friends had originally invested it and the passion with which they had fought for its inception could have had little meaning for the men of whom T. S. Eliot wrote, or indeed for the unemployed of Edwardian England, to whom his words can equally be applied:

No man has hired us.
With pocketed hands
And lowered faces
We stand about in open places
And shiver in unlit rooms.
Only the wind moves
Over empty fields, untilled
Where the plough rests, at an angle
To the furrow. In this land
There shall be one cigarette to two men,
To two women one half pint of bitter
Ale. In this land
No man has hired us.
Our life is unwelcome, our death
Unmentioned in *The Times*.[9]

Notes and references

THE FOLLOWING ABBREVIATIONS are used:

Ann Rep	*Annual Report*
BkL	Beaverbrook Library
BL	Bodleian Library
BLPES	British Library of Political and Economic Science
BM	British Museum
BPP	*British Parliamentary Papers*
EC	Executive Committee
LL	*Labour Leader*
LP	Labour Party
NCL	Nuffield College Library
NLC	National Liberal Club
NLS	National Library of Scotland
PC	Parliamentary Committee
PRO	Public Record Office
RR	*Railway Review*
TLG	*Trades and Labour Gazette*

Chapter 1   The days of the Social Democrats, 1900-4
(pages 13-34)

1 Bosanquet, Helen. *The administration of charitable relief* (1898), 3
2 London, Jack. *The people of the abyss* (Panther edition, 1963), 123
3 For example, 26.5 per cent of the recruits applying at York, Leeds and Sheffield depots between 1897 and 1900 were rejected as unfit. On this generally see Gilbert, Bentley. *The evolution of national insurance in Great Britain* (1966), 21ff
4 Beveridge, William. *Unemployment : a problem of industry* (1909), 148
5 Pease, Edward. *History of the Fabian Society* (2nd edition, 1925), 215
6 Howell, George. *Trade unionism old and new* (1891), 170-205
7 Campbell, D. *The unemployed problem : the socialist solution* (1894)
8 Haw, George. *The life story of Will Crooks MP* (1917), 265-6
9 ILP, *Ann Rep*, 1895, 26

10 *LL*, 9 Feb 1895

11 ILP, *Ann Rep*, 1897, 14

12 *The Times*, 30 Apr 1902

13 *Justice*, 28 June 1902

14 *The Times*, 25 Dec 1902

15 Hobson and Pease had already been investigating unemployment for a Fabian committee. See NCL, Fabian Society, *EC Minutes*, 24 June 1902

16 *LL*, 27 Dec 1902

17 *Daily Mail*, 2 Mar 1903

18 *LL*, 7 Mar 1903

19 A hope expressed in *Justice*, 7 Feb 1903

20 Ibid, 1 Mar 1903

21 Ibid, 29 Nov 1902

22 Ibid, 31 Jan 1903

23 Ibid, 21 Feb 1903

24 *LL*, 21 Feb 1903; *The Times*, 16 Feb 1903

25 *The Times*, 9 Feb 1903

26 Ibid, 26 Feb 1903

27 *Westminster Gazette*, 14 Feb 1903

28 General Union of Operative Carpenters and Joiners, London District Committee, *Half yearly report*, 31 Jan 1903, 1

29 *LL*, 21 Feb 1903

30 Kent Archives Office, Chilston Papers, U 564. CLP 7, ff 10-11. A. Akers-Douglas to Lord Knollys, 12 Feb 1903

31 *Hansard*, 4th series, 118, c137. 18 Feb 1903

32 PRO CAB 37/65. *Unemployed processions*. 22 May 1903

33 SDF, *Ann Rep*, 1903, 17

34 *The Times*, 28 Jan 1903. On the 'impossibilists' generally see Tsuzuki, Chushuchi. 'The impossibilist revolt in Britain', *International Review of Social History*, 1 (1956), 377-97

35 *Justice*, 7 Nov 1903

36 Ibid, 12 Dec 1903

37 Reported in the *Daily Graphic*, 23 Dec 1903

38 *LL*, 19 Sept 1903

39 Ibid, 6 June 1903; 27 June 1903; 25 July 1903; 10 Oct 1903

40 Ibid, 12 Dec 1903

41 Ibid, 9 Jan 1904

42 *The Times*, 7 Nov 1903

43 C/o Mrs J. Clay, Buxton Papers, uncatalogued. L. Maxse to S. Buxton, 26 May 1903

44 *The Times*, 8 Sept 1903
45 Ibid, 12 Apr 1904
46 Ibid. For a full account of this organisation see Brown, Kenneth. 'The Trade Union Tariff Reform Association, 1904-1913, *Journal of British Studies*, 9, No 2 (May 1970), 141-53

Chapter 2   The Unemployed Workmen's Bill, 1904-5 (pages 35-67)

1 *LL*, 20 Feb 1904
2 Ibid, 15 July 1904
3 *Social Democrat*, 8 (July 1904), 392
4 *Justice*, 15 Oct 1904
5 *National Union Gleanings*, 23 (1904), 262
6 See the report in the *Daily News*, 15 Oct 1904
7 *COS Review*, 16 (Nov 1904), 268
8 Hardie, James Keir. 'Dealing with the unemployed: a hint from the past', *Nineteenth Century*, 57 (Jan 1905), 50
9 *Justice*, 22 Oct 1904
10 *Clarion*, 2 Dec 1904
11 *Social Democrat*, 9 (Dec 1904), 720
12 Quoted in Haw, *Will Crooks*, 239-40
13 *Social Democrat*, 9 (Nov 1904), 646-9
14 An incident reported in *Morning Post*, 20 Dec 1904
15 *LL*, 30 Dec 1904
16 *Justice*, 29 Oct 1904
17 The three branches were Bradford, Chorley, and Rawtenstall
18 TUC, *PC Minutes*, 24 Oct 1904
19 Quoted in *National Union Gleanings*, 23 (1904), 268
20 Quoted in Haw, *Will Crooks*, 238-9
21 BM, Balfour Papers, Add MSS 49763, f 14. A. J. Balfour to J. Sandars, 4 Jan 1905
22 SDF, *Ann Rep*, 1905, 17
23 *The Times*, 24 Dec 1904
24 *Justice*, 15 Oct 1904
25 *Daily Graphic*, 19 Dec 1904; *Daily Mail*, 19 Dec 1904
26 *Royal commission on the poor law and the relief of distress, Appendix 8* [Cd 5066] *BPP*, 48 (1910), 69
27 Ibid
28 *Justice*, 19 Nov 1904

M

29 Ibid, 25 Mar 1905
30 BM, Gladstone Papers, Add MSS 41217, ff 134-5. H. Gladstone to H. Campbell-Bannerman, 14 Nov 1904
31 Ibid, Add MSS 46019, f 84. J. Bryce to H. Gladstone, 14 Dec 1904
32 *Daily News*, 15 Feb 1905
33 *LL*, 17 Feb 1905
34 Friendly Society of Ironfounders, *Monthly Report*, Apr 1905, 13
35 *RR*, 17 Feb 1905
36 BM, Balfour Papers, Add MSS 49763, f 73. J. Sandars to A. J. Balfour, 21 Jan 1905
37 PRO CAB 37/74. *The unemployed.* 17 Feb 1905
38 Ibid, 37/75. *The unemployed.* 2 Mar 1905
39 Ibid
40 BM, Balfour Papers, Add MSS 49758, ff 11-12. Lord Salisbury to A. J. Balfour, 5 Mar 1905
41 In two letters to *The Times*, 9 and 17 May 1905
42 BM, Campbell-Bannerman Papers, Add MSS 41238, f 9. S. Buxton to H. Campbell-Bannerman, 16 Jan 1905
43 *Hansard*, 4th series, 144, c 147. 3 Apr 1905
44 Ibid, 145, c 460. 18 Apr 1905
45 *LL*, 28 Apr 1905
46 *RR*, 21 Apr 1905
47 Quoted in *COS Review*, 17 (May 1905), 284
48 *Justice*, 6 May 1905
49 *TLG*, June 1905, 3
50 *Justice*, 22 Apr 1905
51 *TLG*, May 1905, 2
52 *LL*, 28 Apr 1905
53 *Royal commission on the poor law and the relief of distress, Appendix 8* [Cd 5066] *BPP*, 48 (1910), 14
54 *Kentish Gazette*, 14 Oct 1905
55 'W.C. and others very nervous about the Leicester march...' BM, Burns Papers, Add MSS 46323. Diary, 16 May 1905
56 Transport House, LRC Letter Files, 23, f 40, nd
57 BLPES, *ILP Head Office Circular* (unbound), nd
58 *Daily Telegraph*, 16 May 1905
59 *Daily Express*, 18 May 1905
60 BLPES, *ILP Head Office Circular* (unbound), 16 May 1905
61 *LL*, 19 May 1905
62 *Hansard*, 4th series, 166, c 774. 18 May 1905
63 *LL*, 26 May 1905

64 BM, Burns Papers, Add MSS 46323. Diary, 24 May 1905
65 *LL*, 26 May 1905
66 *Daily Graphic*, 21 June 1905
67 *RR*, 23 June 1905
68 *Eltradion*, July 1905, 49
69 *Justice*, 8 July 1905
70 Compiled from reports in *LL* which reported on 21 July 1905 that over 100 meetings had been held
71 *LL*, 7 July 1905
72 *Daily Express*, 10 July 1905
73 *Daily Mail*, 17 July 1905
74 *LL*, 28 July 1905
75 Ibid, 11 Aug 1905
76 *Hansard*, 4th series, 151, c 429. 7 Aug 1905
77 BLPES, collection of early LRC papers bound as *Infancy of the Labour Party*, I, 331. 29 July 1905
78 *Hansard*, 4th series, 150, cc 981-1018. 31 July 1905
79 *LL*, 4 Aug 1905
80 Webb, Beatrice. *Our partnership* (1948), 317. On the question of the commission's appointment see Brown, John. 'The appointment of the 1905 poor law commission', *Bulletin of the Institute of Historical Research*, 42 (Nov 1969), 239-42, and my reply (which, at the time this book went to press, was expected to appear in the *Bulletin* in Nov 1971)
81 *Hansard*, 4th series, 150, c 1348. 2 Aug 1905
82 BM, Balfour Papers, Add MSS 49776, f 37. W. Long to A. J. Balfour, 6 Dec 1904
83 TUC, *Ann Rep*, 1905. *Report of a deputation on unemployment*, 14
84 *Hansard*, 4th series, 145, c 1346. 9 May 1905
85 *Standard*, 5 Aug 1905
86 *LL*, 4 Aug 1905
87 *Typographical Circular*, Sept 1905, 5
88 *Clarion*, 11 Aug 1905
89 *LL*, 8 Sept 1905
90 Transport House, LRC Letter Files, 26, f 95. Memorandum dated 21 Oct 1905
91 *Justice*, 2 Dec 1905
92 BLPES, *ILP NAC Minutes*, 3 Oct 1905
93 Transport House, LRC Letter Files, 26, f 287. J. R. MacDonald to W. S. Sanders, 25 Sept 1905
94 Hardie, James Keir. *John Bull and his unemployed* (1905), 11

M*

95 Quoted in Thompson, Paul. *Socialists, Liberals, and Labour* (1967), 222

96 *Justice*, 18 Nov 1905

97 *Daily Graphic*, 21 Nov 1905

98 *The Times*, 15 Dec 1905

99 BM, Balfour Papers, Add MSS 49858, f 42. A. J. Balfour to Sir F. Younghusband, 21 Nov 1905

100 List of contributors in *Justice*, 2 Dec 1905

Chapter 3   The birth of the Right to Work Bill, 1906-7
                (pages 68-84)

1 *Justice*, 9 Dec 1905

2 *LL*, 9 Dec 1904

3 BLPES, Beveridge Papers, L, I, 203. W. H. Beveridge to his mother, 4 Mar 1905

4 BM, Campbell-Bannerman Papers, Add MSS 41217, f 210. H. Gladstone to H. Campbell-Bannerman, 17 Apr 1905

5 C/o Mrs J. Clay, Buxton Papers, uncatalogued. A. Birrell to S. Buxton, 7 May 1905

6 *LL*, 23 June 1905

7 *The Times*, 17 Nov 1905

8 BL, Asquith Papers, 10, f 173. H. Campbell-Bannerman to H. H. Asquith, 1 Dec 1905

9 *TLG*, Oct 1904, 2; similar suggestions were made in *RR*, 3 Apr 1904, and *Justice*, 4 Apr 1904

10 Quoted in Kent, William. *John Burns : labour's lost leader* (1950), 158

11 *Justice*, 16 Dec 1905

12 *Eltradion*, Dec 1905, 129

13 BM, Burns Papers, Add MSS 46323. Diary, 14 Dec 1905

14 *Standard*, 19 Jan 1906

15 See the candidates' manifestos in NLC, *Election addresses*, 1906

16 Crooks, Will. 'The prospects and programme of the Labour Party', *National Review*, 45 (1906), 627

17 These are the conclusions of Russell, Anthony. *The general election of 1906* (Oxford D Phil thesis, 1962)

18 BL, Asquith Papers, 10, f 200. H. Campbell-Bannerman to H. H. Asquith, 21 Jan 1906

19 BM, Burns Papers, Add MSS 46324. Diary, 1 Feb 1906

20 *The Times*, 15 May 1906
21 A copy survives in BLPES, ILP Watford Branch, Correspondence File 1, f 37. 16 May 1906
22 Montefiore, Dora. *From a Victorian to a modern* (1927), 59
23 C/o Mrs J. Clay, Buxton Papers, uncatalogued. Lord Ripon to S. Buxton, 28 May 1906
24 BM, Ripon Papers, Add MSS 43555, f 255. S. Buxton to Lord Ripon, 27 May 1906
25 BM, Burns Papers, Add MSS 46324. Diary, 27 June 1906
26 BLPES, Passfield Papers, I, 1, Vol 25. B. Webb Diary, 9 Feb 1906
27 BM, Campbell-Bannerman Papers, Add MSS 41207, ff 50-1. H. Campbell-Bannerman to Lord Knollys, 13 Feb 1906
28 BM, Burns Papers, Add MSS 46324. Diary, 12 May 1906
29 *Reynold's Newspaper*, 8 July 1906
30 *Justice*, 21 July 1906
31 *Reynold's Newspaper*, 15 July 1906
32 *TLG*, Sept 1906, 18
33 *Reynold's Newspaper*, 2 July 1906
34 Amalgamated Society of Engineers, *Monthly Journal*, Aug 1906, 6
35 *RR*, 27 July 1906
36 *The Times*, 6 Oct 1906
37 Amalgamated Society of Engineers, *Monthly Journal*, Aug 1906, 5-6
38 *Hansard*, 4th series, 171, c 1861. 27 Mar 1907
39 Ibid, 169, c 107. 12 Feb 1907
40 ILP, *Ann Rep*, 1907, 53
41 *LL*, 1 Mar 1907
42 *Hansard*, 4th series, 171, c 1859. 27 Mar 1907
43 *Justice*, 26 Jan 1907
44 *Hansard*, 4th series, 171, cc 1859-60. 27 Mar 1907
45 BM, Burns Papers, Add MSS 46325. Diary, 13 Apr 1907
46 Burns, John. *The unemployed* (1893), 17
47 *Hansard*, 4th series, 171, c 1853. 27 Mar 1907
48 National Amalgamated Union of Labour, *Quarterly Report*, 30 Mar 1907
49 A Bill to promote work through public authorities for unemployed persons. 7 Edw VII, c 3
50 These are the conclusions of Brown, John. *Ideas concerning social policy and their influence on legislation in Britain, 1902-1911* (London PhD thesis, 1964)
51 *LL*, 16 Aug 1907
52 Ibid, 19 July 1907

Chapter 4   The battle for the Right to Work Bill, 1907-8
             (pages 85-112)

 1 BM, Burns Papers, Add MSS 46325. Diary, 9 July 1907
 2 See MacDonald's speech introducing the Bill in *Hansard*, 4th series,
    177, c 1446. 9 July 1907
 3 BM, Ripon Papers, Add MSS 43555, ff 266-7. S. Buxton to Lord
    Ripon, 19 Aug 1907
 4 MacDonald, James Ramsay. *The new Unemployed Bill of the Lab-
    our Party* (1907)
 5 Quoted in Thompson, Laurence. *Robert Blatchford, portrait of an
    Englishman* (1951), 185
 6 *LL*, 11 Oct 1907
 7 Ibid, 1 Nov 1907
 8 Ibid, 13 Dec 1907
 9 *Clarion*, 17 Jan 1908
10 *LL*, 7 Feb 1908
11 *Typographical Circular*, Feb 1908, 10
12 BLPES, *Infancy of the Labour Party*, II, 73. 10 Feb 1908
13 LP. *The Labour Party and unemployment* (1908)
14 BM, Burns Papers, Add MSS 46326. Diary, 11 Mar 1908
15 BL, Asquith Papers, 5, f 14. H. H. Asquith to the King, 11 Mar 1908
16 BM, Ripon Papers, Add MSS 43555, f 273. S. Buxton to Lord Ripon,
    4 Mar 1908
17 Ibid, f 276. Lord Ripon to S. Buxton, 6 Mar 1908
18 PRO CAB 37/91. *The Unemployed Workmen Bill*. 9 Mar 1908
19 Bristol Right to Work Committee, *Ann Rep*, 1908, 2
20 Masterman, Charles. 'Politics in transition', *Nineteenth Century*, 62
    (Jan 1908), 16-17
21 Cox, Harold. 'The right to work', *Quarterly Review*, 202 (Jan 1908),
    203
22 *The Times*, 14 Mar 1908
23 *Daily Mail*, 13 Mar 1908
24 *Standard*, 12 Mar 1908
25 The Liberal member for Watford, for example, told the local branch
    of the ILP that MacDonald's stand had decided his own hostile vote.
    BLPES, ILP Watford Branch, Correspondence File 2, f 33. 13 Mar
    1908
26 A censure motion moved on Maddison and Vivian at the 1908 TUC
    congress was passed, however, by a surprisingly small margin,
    826,000 to 821,000. TUC, *Ann Rep*, 1908, 135

27 Raine, George. *Present-day socialism* (1908), 130
28 *Daily Telegraph*, 14 Mar 1908
29 *Daily Graphic*, 19 Mar 1908
30 *LL*, 20 Mar 1908
31 TUC, *Ann Rep*, 1908, 123
32 *LL*, 8 May 1908
33 *The Times*, 20 Apr 1908
34 Churchill, Randolph. *Winston S. Churchill. II. Young statesman, 1901-1914* (1967), 240-4
35 BL, Asquith Papers, 11, f 89. J. Burns to H. H. Asquith, 13 Apr 1908
36 Ibid, ff 95-6. C. F. G. Masterman to H. H. Asquith, 13 Apr 1908
37 ILP, *Ann Rep*, 1908, 60
38 *LL*, 29 May 1908
39 *Justice*, 25 July 1908
40 *LL*, 7 Aug 1908
41 *Daily Graphic*, 19 Sept 1908
42 *LL*, 25 Sept 1908
43 *New Age*, 3 Oct 1908
44 TUC, *Ann Rep*, 1908, 165
45 *Justice*, 15 June 1907
46 Ibid, 24 Oct 1908
47 Ibid, 10 Oct 1908
48 BM, Gladstone Papers, Add MSS 45994, ff 164-5. M. L. Walter to H. Gladstone, 10 Oct 1908
49 Masterman, Lucy. *C. F. G. Masterman* (1939), 110-11
50 *Justice*, 30 Mar 1907; SDF, *Ann Rep*, 1907, 17
51 National Union of Gas Workers and General Labourers, *Minutes of Delegate Meeting*, 17 Oct 1908
52 *Clarion*, 23 Oct 1908
53 *Justice*, 24 Oct 1908
54 PRO CAB 37/95. *The unemployed*, 17 Oct 1908
55 BM, Burns Papers, Add MSS 46326. Diary, 20 Oct 1908
56 Masterman, *Masterman*, 112
57 BM, Burns Papers, Add MSS 46326. Diary, 21 Oct 1908
58 *Standard*, 5 Dec 1908
59 *Hansard*, 4th series, 195, c 46. 27 Oct 1908
60 Ibid, 196, c 296. 11 Nov 1908
61 Ibid, c 270. 11 Nov 1908
62 Ibid, c 713. 13 Nov 1908
63 Ibid, c 1776. 23 Nov 1908
64 Ibid, 195, c 47. 27 Oct 1908

65 Ibid, 196, c 46. 10 Nov 1908
66 Ibid, cc 640-4. 12 Nov 1908
67 BM, Burns Papers, Add MSS 46326. Diary, 12 Nov 1908
68 TUC, *PC Minutes*, 9 Dec. 1908
69 *Hansard*, 4th series, 198, c 1252. 14 Dec 1908
70 *Standard*, 6 Feb 1909
71 *The Times*, 22 Jan 1909
72 *Daily Mail*, 22 Jan 1909
73 *Hansard*, 5th series, 1, cc 98-9. 17 Feb 1909
74 *Justice*, 23 Jan 1909
75 *LL*, 5 Mar 1909
76 Ibid, 12 Mar 1909
77 *Clarion*, 3 Apr 1909
78 *Justice*, 7 Feb 1909
79 Ibid, 31 Oct 1908
80 *LL*, 20 Nov 1908
81 *Typographical Circular*, Nov 1908, 11
82 *Clarion*, 12 Mar 1909

Chapter 5   The decline of the 'right to work', 1909
(pages 113-130)

1   *Hansard*, 5th series, 1, c 184, 17 Feb 1909
2   Masterman, *Masterman*, 128
3   *Social Democrat*, 13 (Apr 1909), 171
4   *Justice*, 27 Nov 1909
5   *LL*, 9 Apr 1909
6   *Morning Post*, 1 May 1909
7   For Example, *The Times*, 1 May 1909; *Westminster Gazette*, 1 May 1909; *Daily Graphic*, 1 May 1909
8   National Union of Boot and Shoe Operatives, *Monthly Report*, May 1909, 223
9   *Typographical Circular*, May 1909, 2
10 ILP, *Ann Rep*, 1909, 21
11 *Clarion*, 20 Mar 1908
12 *LL*, 10 Jan 1908
13 *The Times*, 25 Jan 1909
14 *Socialist Review*, 3 (June 1909), 246
15 *The Times*, 16 Jan 1909
16 *Hansard*, 5th series, 1 cc 54-5. 16 Feb 1909

17 *LL*, 26 Feb 1909

18 BLPES, ILP, *Minutes and Reports from Head Office*, July 1909

19 *Socialist Review*, 4 (Nov 1909), 175

20 *Hansard*, 5th series, 10, cc 983-4. 6 Sept 1909

21 *LL*, 12 Sept 1912

22 LP, *Ann Rep*, 1909, 93

23 BLPES, Beveridge Papers, D 026. Unemployment Insurance: criticisms. Dec 1909

24 Quoted in Muggeridge, Kitty, and Adam, Ruth. *Beatrice Webb. A life* (1967), 189

25 BLPES, Passfield Papers, I, 1, Vol 26. B. Webb Diary, 30 Jan 1908

26 ILP, *Ann Rep*, 1909, 45

27 A point stressed by Quelch when he debated the report with Lansbury in 1910. See *Justice*, 1 Oct 1910

28 Reported in Associated Shipwrights Society, *Quarterly Report*, Mar 1909, 23-6

29 BLPES, ILP, *Minutes and Reports from Head Office*, July 1909

30 *Ibid*, Apr 1909

31 *LL*, 29 May 1908

32 *Fabian News*, 20 (Apr 1909), 40

33 ILP, *Ann Rep*, 1909, 71

34 *LL*, 4 June 1909

35 *Hansard*, 5th series, 5, c 519. 19 May 1909

36 TUC, *PC Minutes*, 11 July 1909

37 BLPES, Beveridge Papers, L, I, 204. W. H. Beveridge to his mother, 7 July 1909

38 TUC, *PC Minutes*, 11 July 1909

39 National Free Labour Association, *Ann Rep*, 1909, 40

40 *LL*, 25 June 1909

41 National Amalgamated Union of Labour, *Quarterly Report*, June 1909, 4-5

42 National Union of Boot and Shoe Operatives, *Monthly Report*, Mar 1909, 158-9

43 TUC, *Ann Rep*, 1909, 150-2

44 TUC. *PC Minutes*, 11 July 1909

45 *Hansard*, 5th series, 6, cc 100-102. 16 June 1909

46 *LL*, 19 Feb 1909

47 Ibid, 26 Mar 1909

48 *Socialist Review*, 3 (June 1909), 256

Chapter 6 . A wasted year, 1910
(pages 131-140)

1 NLC, *Election addresses,* Jan 1910
2 Belcher in the *Socialist Review,* 4 (Jan 1910), 336; Barnes in ibid, 4 (Dec 1909), 262
3 *LL,* 11 Feb 1910
4 Ibid, 4 Mar 1910
5 Clarion, 21 Jan 1910
6 BLPES, Beveridge Papers, L, 3, 225. H. R. Maynard to W. H. Beveridge, 2 Feb 1910
7 BL, Asquith Papers, 5, f 190. H. H. Asquith to the King, 22 Feb 1910
8 *LL,* 11 Mar 1910
9 Ibid, 4 Mar 1910
10 NLS, Elibank Papers, MSS 8802, ff 51-2. J. R. MacDonald to Master of Elibank, 13 Apr 1910
11 *LL,* 18 Mar 1910
12 Ibid
13 Ibid
14 BkL, Lloyd George Papers, C/5/11/1A. J. R. MacDonald to D. Lloyd George, nd
15 *LL,* 26 Aug 1910
16 Ibid, 17 Oct 1910
17 Ibid, 4 Feb 1910
18 *TLG,* Feb 1910, 3
19 GFTU, *Annual General Council Meeting,* 2 July 1910, 29
20 Joint Board, *Minutes,* 28 June 1910
21 *LL,* 3 June 1910
22 Blewett, Neal. *The British general elections of 1910* (Oxford D Phil thesis 1966), 575 ff
23 NLC, *Election addresses,* Dec 1910
24 *LL,* 24 June 1910
25 *Hansard,* 5th series, 16, c 819. 8 Apr 1910
26 *Clarion,* 17 Feb 1911
27 BLPES, Beveridge Papers, L, I, 205. W. H. Beveridge to his mother, 24 Jan 1910
28 Tallents, Stephen. *Man and boy* (1943), 178
29 *Justice,* 24 Sept 1910
30 Beveridge, William. 'Labour exchanges in the United Kingdom ', *Conference Internationale du chomâge, Rapport No 26,* Sept 1910

31 TUC, *8th Quarterly Report of the PC,* **48-50**
32 TUC, *Ann Rep,* 1911, 190-2

Chapter 7   National Insurance and beyond, 1911-14
             (pages 141-163)

1 *LL,* 17 Feb 1911
2 Ibid, 24 Mar 1911
3 Ibid, 17 Feb 1911
4 Ibid, 24 Feb 1911
5 Ibid, 10 Mar 1911
6 Ibid, 5 May 1911
7 *Socialist Review,* 6 (Apr 1911) 87-8
8 *Hansard,* 5th series, 25, c 1219. 10 May 1911
9 *Justice,* 20 May 1911
10 Newcastle University Library, Runciman Papers, Box 12. W. S. Churchill to W. Runciman, July 1909
11 C/o Mrs J. Clay, Buxton Papers, uncatalogued. H. Llewellyn Smith to S. Buxton, 24 Jan 1911, complained about these difficulties
12 Ibid. Unemployment Insurance Memorandum, 16 Mar 1911
13 Ibid. S. Buxton to D. Lloyd George, nd. Buxton said that this was 'endangering the scheme' and added that ' there would be great disappointment, therefore, if the proportion of the State's contribution ... were reduced ... it would make the scheme unworkable'.
14 *Typographical Circular,* June 1911, 10
15 *Hansard,* 5th series, 32, c 827. 30 Nov 1911
16 Ibid, 31, cc 2108-20. 16 Nov 1911
17 Ibid, 26, c 477. 25 May 1911
18 Reported in Amalgamated Toolmakers' Society, *Amalgamated Toolmakers' Monthly,* July 1911, 10-13
19 BLPES, ILP, *Minutes and Reports from Head Office,* 31 May 1911
20 BLPES, Passfield Papers, I, 1, Vol 25. B. Webb Diary, 13 May 1911
21 Amalgamated Society of Carpenters and Joiners, *Monthly Report,* July 1911, 304
22 *The Times,* 31 July 1911
23 BLPES, BSP Papers, f 4. Newscutting, Sept 1911
24 *Justice,* 13 May 1911
25 NCL, Fabian Society Collection, Part A, Box 4, Correspondence from S. Webb. S. Webb to W. S. Sanders, 17 May 1911
26 BLPES, Passfield Papers, II, 4e, ff 33-4. G. Lansbury to S. Webb, 24 May 1911

27 *Justice*, 27 May 1911
28 *LL*, 9 June 1911
29 Ibid, 16 June 1911
30 Ibid, 23 and 30 June 1911
31 Amalgamated Society of Engineers, *Monthly Journal*, July 1911, 5-6
32 BLPES, Herbert Bryan Papers, General Correspondence Va, f 17. H. Duberry to H. Bryan, 13 July 1911
33 *Hansard*, 5th series, 27, c 1462. 6 July 1911
34 BLPES, *Infancy of the Labour Party*, II, 204. 14 July 1911
35 *LL*, 21 July 1911
36 BLPES, Beveridge Papers, L, I, 205. W. H. Beveridge to his mother, 6 Aug 1911
37 Hamilton, Mary. *Arthur Henderson. A biography* (1938), 73-4
38 Riddell, Lord. *More pages from my diary, 1908-1914* (1934), 21
39 BLPES, Passfield Papers, II, 4e, f 72e. W. A. Colegate to B. Webb, 18 Aug 1911
40 BkL, Lloyd George Papers, C/6/5/5. Master of Elibank to D. Lloyd George, 5 Oct 1911
41 BLPES, Beveridge Papers, L, I, 205. W. H. Beveridge to his mother, 15 Aug 1911
42 BLPES, Passfield Papers, II, 4e, f 64a. M. Reeves to B. Webb, 3 Aug 1911
43 TUC, *Ann Rep*, 1911, 204-8
44 BLPES, Passfield Papers, II, 4e, f 103c. C. D. Sharp to B. Webb, 20 Sept 1911
45 NLS, Elibank Papers, MSS 8802, f 334. J. R. MacDonald to the Master of Elibank, 4 Oct 1911
46 *LL*, 8 Dec 1911
47 BLPES, BSP Papers, f 4. Newscutting, Sept 1911
48 *The Times*, 27 Oct 1911
49 BLPES, Lansbury Papers, IV, f 231. E. C. Fairchild to G. Lansbury, 25 Oct 1911
50 NLS, Elibank Papers, MSS 8802, f 337. J. R. MacDonald to the Master of Elibank, 9 Oct 1911
51 *Daily News*, 10 Oct 1911
52 *LL*, 20 Oct 1911
53 BLPES, Passfield Papers, II, 4e, f 150. C. M. Lloyd to B. Webb, 6 Nov 1911
54 *Hansard*, 5th series, 32, cc 1419-1530. 6 Dec 1911
55 *LL*, 24 Nov 1911
56 Ibid, 1 Dec 1911

57 Ibid, 15 Dec 1911
58 Ibid, 8 Dec 1911
59 Ibid, 26 Jan 1912
60 *Hansard*, 5th series, 50, c 1324. 24 Mar 1913
61 Ibid, 42, c 1599. 18 Oct 1912
62 TUC, *Ann Rep*, 1912, 219
63 National Amalgamated Union of Labour, *Quarterly Report*, June 1913, 4; see also Fyrth, Hubert, and Collins, Henry. *The foundry workers* (1968), 134
64 Operative Bricklayers Society, *Ann Rep*, 1912, 111
65 Pelling, Henry. *Politics and society in late Victorian Britain* (1968), 153
66 On this generally see Pelling, op cit, 152 ff
67 ILP, *Ann Rep*, 1912, 66
68 Ibid, 9
69 Ibid, 1913, 42-3
70 *LL*, 25 Feb 1912

Chapter 8   Conclusions
            (pages 164-174)

1 Tressall, Robert. *The ragged trousered philanthropists* (Penguin edition, 1940), 33
2 Sanders, William. *Early socialist days* (1927), 18
3 Masterman, Charles. *From the abyss* (1901), 14
4 LRC, *Ann Rep*, 1903, 12. There were also 835 Fabians affiliated. For SDF membership see Kendall, Walter. *The revolutionary movement in Britain, 1900-1921* (1969), 311
5 Brotherton Library University of Leeds, A. Mattison Papers, Notebook B, 11. 14 Jan 1912
6 Bailey, George. 'The right to work', *Westminster Review*, 170 Dec 1908), 618
7 Quoted in Pelling, Henry. *A short history of the Labour Party* (2nd ed 1965), 21
8 BLPES, Passfield Papers, I, 1, Vol 27. B. Webb Diary, 30 Nov 1910
9 Eliot, T. S. Choruses from 'The Rock'. Reprinted by permission of Faber & Faber Ltd and Harcourt Brace and Jovanovich from *Collected Poems 1909-62*

TABLE 1

Unemployment 1900-14 : percentages of all trade unions making returns

	Jan	Feb	Mar	Apr	May	June	July	Aug	Sept	Oct	Nov	Dec
1900	2.3	2.4	2.0	2.0	1.9	2.1	2.2	2.5	3.0	2.8	2.7	3.5
1901	3.5	3.4	3.1	3.4	3.0	3.0	2.9	3.4	3.2	3.2	3.3	4.2
1902	4.0	3.9	3.2	3.4	3.5	3.7	3.5	4.0	4.5	4.5	4.4	5.0
1903	4.9	4.3	3.9	4.6	3.5	3.9	4.4	5.0	5.2	5.6	5.5	6.3
1904	6.1	5.6	5.5	5.5	5.8	5.5	5.6	5.9	6.3	6.3	6.5	7.1
1905	6.3	5.7	5.2	5.2	4.7	4.8	4.7	4.9	4.8	4.6	4.3	4.5
1906	4.3	4.1	3.4	3.2	3.1	3.2	3.1	3.3	3.3	3.9	4.0	4.4
1907	3.9	3.5	3.2	2.8	3.0	3.1	3.2	3.6	4.1	4.2	4.5	5.6
1908	5.8	6.0	6.4	7.1	7.4	7.9	7.9	8.5	9.3	9.5	8.7	9.1
1909	8.7	8.4	8.2	8.2	7.9	7.9	7.9	7.7	7.4	7.1	6.5	6.6
1910	6.8	5.7	5.2	4.4	4.2	3.7	3.8	4.0	4.3	4.4	4.6	5.0
1911	3.9	3.3	3.0	2.8	2.5	3.0	2.9	3.3	2.9	2.8	2.6	3.1
1912	2.7	2.8	11.3*	3.6	2.7	2.5	2.6	2.2	2.1	2.0	1.8	2.3
1913	2.2	2.0	1.9	1.7	1.9	1.9	1.9	2.0	2.3	2.2	2.0	2.6
1914	2.5	2.3	2.1	2.1	2.3	2.4	2.8	7.1	5.9	4.4	2.9	2.5

(* distorted by the coal strike)

Board of Trade, *Seventeenth abstract of labour statistics* [Cd 7733]
BPP, 61 (1914-16), 322

TABLE 2   **191**

TABLE 2

Right to Work Committees and their source of reference

LONDON BOROUGHS

Battersea	*The Times*, 6 Nov 1908
Bermondsey	Ibid, 5 Nov 1908
*Canning Town	*TLG*, Sept 1908, 9
Finsbury	*Justice*, 7 Nov 1908
Hackney	Ibid, 28 Nov 1908
*Hammersmith	Ibid
Islington	*LL*, 30 Oct 1908
Lambeth	*Justice*, 27 Feb 1909
St Pancras	*The Times*, 23 Dec 1908
*Southwark	*Justice*, 19 Dec 1908
Willesden	Ibid, 9 Nov 1907
Woolwich	*Woolwich Labour Representation Association Minutes*, 24 Nov 1908

PROVINCIAL

*Aberdeen	*TLG*, Sept 1908, 9
Accrington	*Justice*, 2 Dec 1905
Arbroath	Ibid
Barking	Ibid
Birmingham	Ibid
Blackpool	Ibid, 17 Mar 1906
*Bradford	*TLG*, Oct 1908, 10
Bristol	Bristol Right to Work Committee, *Annual Report*
Bury	*Justice*, 2 Dec 1905
Coventry	Ibid, 24 Oct 1908
Croydon	*The Times*, 26 Oct 1908
Doncaster	*TLG*, Nov 1908, 12
East Ham	*Justice*, 2 Dec 1905
Edinburgh	*TLG*, Oct 1907, 11
Erith	*Justice*, 28 Nov 1908
Gorton	Ibid, 17 Feb 1906
Govan	Ibid, 2 Dec 1905
*Halifax	*TLG*, Nov 1908, 12

TABLE **2**

Leeds	*Justice*, 2 Dec 1905
Leicester	*LL*, 8 Dec 1905
Lincoln	*Justice*, 27 Feb 1909
Liverpool	Ibid, 24 Jan 1906
Longton	Ibid, 2 Dec 1905
Manchester	Ibid
Middleton	Ibid, 17 Mar 1906
Newark	Ibid, 2 Dec 1905
Newcastle	Ibid
Newport	*LL*, 6 Nov 1908
Nottingham	*Justice*, 2 Dec 1908
Orpington	Ibid, 19 Dec 1908
Oxford	Ibid, 2 Dec 1908
Partick	Ibid
*Reading	Ibid, 24 Oct 1908
St Mary Cray	Ibid, 19 Dec 1908
Southampton	Ibid, 17 Oct 1908
Stoke	Ibid, 2 Dec 1905
Swansea	Ibid
Watford	Ibid
West Ham	Ibid
Wigan	Ibid
*Wolverhampton	*TLG*, Oct 1908, 10
York	*Justice*, 2 Dec 1905

(* committees formed in response to Smith appeal in 1908)

Biographical notes

THESE NOTES COVER most of the important people mentioned in the text. They are not meant to be exhaustive and most of the entries refer only to the years spanned by the book. Further information can be found in almost every case by consulting the *Dictionary of National Biography* or *Who Was Who*.

Akers-Douglas, Henry (1851-1926)	Conservative MP 1880-1911. Chief Commissioner of Works 1895-1902. Home Secretary 1902-5
Alden, Percy (1865-1944)	Warden of Mansfield House University Settlement 1891-1901. Liberal MP for Tottenham 1906-18
Asquith, Herbert (1852-1928)	Liberal MP for East Fife 1886-1918. Chancellor of the Exchequer 1905-8. Prime Minister 1908-16
Balfour, Arthur (1848-1930)	Entered Parliament 1874. Cabinet rank 1886. Conservative Prime Minister 1902-5. Leader of Conservative opposition in the Commons 1905-11
Balfour, Gerald (1853-1943)	Conservative MP for Central Leeds 1885-1906. President of the Local Government Board 1905
Barnes, George (1859-1940)	Secretary Amalgamated Society of Engineers 1896-1908. Labour MP for Blackfriars division of Glasgow 1906-22. Chairman of the Labour Party 1910-11
Beveridge, William (1879-1963) which he designed, in 1910	Economist and civil servant. Made director of the labour exchange system,

Birrell, Augustine
(1850-1933)
Entered Parliament 1889. Liberal MP for North Bristol 1906-18. President of the Board of Education 1905-7. Chief Secretary for Ireland 1907-16

Blatchford, Robert
(1851-1943)
Journalist and socialist. Founder and editor of the *Clarion*

Blumenfeld, Ralph
(1864-1948)
American journalist. Editor of the *Daily Express* 1902-32. Helped found the Anti-Socialist Union in 1908

Bondfield, Margaret
(1873-1953)
Official in the shop assistants' union. Member of the ILP executive 1913-19

Booth, Charles
(1840-1916)
Shipowner and writer on social problems. Served on the poor law commission of 1905-9

Bosanquet, Helen
(1848-1923)
Noted social worker connected with the COS. Served on the poor law commission of 1905-9

Bowerman, Charles
(1851-1947)
General Secretary of the London Society of Compositors 1892-1906. Labour MP for Deptford 1906-31. Secretary of the TUC 1911-23

Brace, William
(1865-1947)
Miners' agent. President of the South Wales Miners' Federation 1911-19. Labour MP for Glamorgan South 1906-18

Broadhurst, Henry
(1840-1911)
Secretary of the Labour Representation League 1873. Secretary of TUC 1875. Liberal MP 1880-92, 1894-1906

Bryce, John
(1838-1922)
Liberal MP 1880-1906. British ambassador in Washington 1907-13

Burns, John
(1858-1943)
Member of the SDF 1884-9. Independent Labour MP for Battersea 1892-1918. President of the Local Government Board 1905-14. President of the Board of Trade 1914. Resigned on the outbreak of war

Buxton, Sidney
(1853-1934)

Entered Parliament as a Liberal 1883. MP for Poplar 1886-1914. Postmaster General 1905-10. President of Board of Trade 1910-14

Campbell-Bannerman, Henry
(1836-1908)

Entered Parliament 1868. Liberal Prime Minister 1905-8

Chamberlain, Joseph
(1836-1914)

Liberal President of the Local Government Board 1886. Joined Conservative cabinet 1895. Resigned as Colonial Secretary in 1903 to launch tariff reform campaign. Crippled by a stroke in 1906

Chandler, Francis
(1849-1937)

General Secretary of the Amalgamated Society of Carpenters and Joiners 1888-1919. Parliamentary Committee of the TUC 1901-4, 1905-11. Member of the poor law commission 1905-9

Churchill, Winston
(1874-1965)

Entered Parliament as a Conservative in 1900. Crossed the floor over tariff reform issue and served as Under-Secretary for the colonies 1905-8. President of the Board of Trade 1908-10. Home Secretary 1910-11. First Lord of the Admiralty 1911-15

Clynes, John
(1869-1949)

Member of the National Union of Gas Workers and General Labourers. Labour MP for North East Manchester 1906-31

Crooks, Will
(1852-1921)

Mayor of Poplar 1901. Labour MP for Woolwich 1903-18

Curran, Pete
(1860-1910)

General organiser of the gas workers and general labourers union. Chairman of the GFTU. Labour MP for Jarrow 1907-10

196   BIOGRAPHICAL NOTES

Davis, William   General Secretary of the brassworkers'
(1848-1923)   union 1872-83, and 1889-1920. Parlia-
                        mentary Committee of the TUC 1881-
                        3, 1896-1902, 1903-20

Duncan, Charles   Members of the engineers' union. Sec-
(1865-1933)   retary of the Workers' Union 1900-28.
                        Labour MP for Barrow 1906-18, and
                        1922-33

Elibank, Master of   Entered Parliament as a Liberal 1900.
(1870-1920)   Scottish whip 1906-10. Parliamentary
                        Secretary to the Treasury 1910-12

Fels, Joseph   American soap manufacturer. Promot-
(1854-1914)   er of vacant lot farming in Britain and
                        America. Became an ardent advocate
                        of the 'single tax' after 1905

George, David Lloyd   Liberal MP 1890-1945. President of
(1863-1945)   the Board of Trade 1905-8. Chancellor
                        of the Exchequer 1908-15

Gill, Alfred   Secretary of Bolton spinners and Lab-
(1856-1914)   our MP for Bolton 1906-14

Gladstone, Herbert   Liberal MP for West Leeds 1885-1910.
(1854-1930)   Chief whip 1899-1905. Home Secre-
                        tary 1905-10

Glasier, John Bruce   Socialist propagandist. Chairman of
(1859-1920)   the ILP 1900-1903. Editor of the *Lab-
                        our Leader* 1904-9

Gooch, George   Historian. Liberal MP for Bath 1906-
(1873-1968)   10

Graham, R. B.   Liberal MP 1886-92. Became an ard-
Cunninghame   ent follower of the socialist William
(1852-1936)   Morris

Grayson, Victor   Theology student and journalist. Won
(1882-?)   Colne Valley by-election as a socialist
                        in 1907. Lost the seat in 1910. Helped
                        to form the BSP in 1911. Left Britain

	in 1914. Place and date of death have not been established
Grey, Edward (1862-1935)	Liberal MP 1885-1916. Foreign Secretary 1905-16
Harcourt, Lewis (1863-1922)	Liberal MP for Rossendale 1904-17. First Commissioner of Works 1905-10, 1915-17
Hardie, James Keir (1856-1915)	Founder of the *Labour Leader* 1889. Founder and Chairman of the ILP 1893-1900, 1913-15. Labour MP 1892-5, 1900-1915. Leader of the Parliamentary Labour Party 1906-8
Henderson, Arthur (1863-1935)	Labour MP for Barnard Castle 1903-18. Chairman of Labour Party 1908-10, and Party Secretary 1911-34
Hill, Octavia (1838-1912)	COS worker with special interest in housing. Member of the poor law commission of 1905-9
Hobson, Samuel (1864-1940)	Irish journalist who helped found the ILP. On the executive of the Fabian Society 1900-1909. Became a guild socialist
Hodge, John (1855-1937)	General Secretary of the British Steel Smelters' Amalgamated Association 1886-1918. Parliamentary Committee of the TUC 1892-4, 1895-6. Member of the Labour Party executive 1906-23. Labour MP for Gorton 1906-23
Hudson, Walter (1852-1935)	Secretary of the Irish branch of the Amalgamated Society of Railway Servants. Labour MP for Newcastle 1906-18
Hyndman, Henry (1842-1921)	Educated at Cambridge. Moving spirit behind the Democratic Federation, which became the SDF in 1884, and he remained as its chairman for many

N

Jowett, Fred (1864-1944)	years. First chairman of the BSP 1911 Twice chairman of the ILP. Labour MP for West Bradford 1906-18
Lansbury, George (1859-1940)	Served on the Poplar Board of Guardians 1892. Member of the poor law commission 1905-9. Labour MP for Bow and Bromley 1910-12, 1922-40
Lee, Henry (1865-1932)	Secretary of the SDF 1885-1911. Secretary of the BSP 1911-13. Editor of *Justice* 1913-24
Loch, Charles (1849-1923)	Secretary of COS 1875-1914. Largely responsible for the majority report of the poor law commission
Long, Walter (1854-1924)	Conservative MP 1880-1921. Parliamentary Secretary to the Local Government Board 1886-92. President of the Local Government Board 1900-1905, 1915-16
Macarthur, Mary (1880-1927)	Women's labour organiser and member of the ILP
Macdonald, James (1857-1938)	Member of the SDF executive. Editor of the *London Trades and Labour Gazette*. Sometime secretary of the London Trades Council
MacDonald, James Ramsay (1866-1937)	Early member of the Fabian Society, the SDF and ILP. First Secretary of the Labour Party 1900-1912. Labour MP for Leicester 1906-18
Mann, Tom (1855-1941)	Member of the SDF and the Amalgamated Society of Engineers. First President of the Dockers' Union 1889-93. Later became a leader of the English syndicalist movement
Masterman, Charles (1873-1927)	Liberal MP for North West Ham 1906-11, South West Bethnal Green 1911-

14. Under-Secretary to the Local Government Board 1908-9. Under-Secretary to the Home Office 1909-12. Financial Secretary to the Treasury 1912

Mitchell, Isaac
(1867-1952)
Trade Unionist. Member of the TUC Parliamentary Committee 1897-8. Secretary of the GFTU 1899-1907. Joined the Labour Department of the Board of Trade 1907

O'Grady, James
(1866-1934)
Furniture worker and Labour MP for East Leeds 1906-18. Member of the ILP

Parker, James
(1865-1942)
Member of the ILP and Labour MP for Halifax 1906-18

Pease, Edward
(1857-1955)
Founder member of the LRC. Founder member and Secretary of Fabian Society

Provis, Samuel
(1845-1926)
Permanent Secretary to the Local Government Board 1898-1910

Quelch, Harry
(1858-1913)
Early member of the SDF. Editor of *Justice*, 1887-1912. Chairman of the London Trades Council 1904-6, 1910-13

Richards, Thomas F.
(1863-1942)
A national organiser of the boot and shoe operatives' union. Labour MP for Wolverhampton 1906-10

Ripon, Lord
(1827-1909)
Entered Parliament 1853. Lord Privy Seal and Liberal leader in the House of Lords 1905-8

Roberts, George
(1869-1928)
A member of the typographers' union. Labour MP for Norwich 1906-18

Runciman, Walter
(1870-1949)
Shipowner. Liberal MP. Parliamentary Secretary to the Local Government Board 1905-7. President of the Board of Education 1908-11

Samuel, Herbert   Liberal MP for Cleveland 1902-18.
(1870-1963)   Postmaster General 1910-14

Seddon, James   One-time President of shop assistants'
(1868-1939)   union. Labour MP for Newton 1906-
                            10

Sexton, James   Secretary of the National Union of
(1856-1938)   Dock Labourers 1893-1922. President
                            of the TUC 1905

Shackleton, David   Labour MP for Clitheroe 1902-10.
(1863-1938)   Member of the TUC Parliamentary
                            Committee 1904-10 and its President
                            1908-9. Labour Party Chairman 1905.
                            Appointed Labour adviser to Home
                            Office in 1910

Shaw, George Bernard   Playwright. Member of the Fabian
(1856-1950)   Society

Sinclair, Archibald   Liberal MP 1892. Assistant private
(1860-1925)   secretary to Campbell-Bannerman
                            1897-1908. Secretary for Scotland 1905-
                            12

Smith, Frank   Journalist and one-time Salvation
(1854-1940)   Army Commissioner. ILP member of
                            the London County Council 1892-5,
                            1898-1901, 1907-13

Snowden, Philip   ILP propagandist. Chairman of the
(1864-1937)   ILP 1903-6. Labour MP for Blackburn
                            1906-18

Spencer, Lord   Liberal MP 1857. Cabinet rank 1880.
(1835-1910)   Liberal leader in the House of Lords
                            1902. Incapacitated by illness in 1905

Summerbell, Tom   Member of the ILP. Labour MP for
(1861-1910)   Sunderland 1906-10

Thorne, Will   Member of the SDF. A founder of the
(1857-1946)   gas workers and general labourers'
                            union, and its General Secretary 1889-

1934. Parliamentary Committee of the TUC 1894-1933. Labour MP for West Ham 1906-45

Tillett, Ben (1860-1943)
A founder of the dockers' union and its Secretary until 1922

Trevelyan, Charles (1870-1958)
Liberal MP 1899-1918. Parliamentary Charity Commissioner 1906-8. Parliamentary Secretary to the Board of Education 1908-14

Turner, Ben (1863-1942)
President of the General Union of Weavers and Textile Workers 1902-22

Tweedmouth, Lord (1849-1909)
Entered Parliament as a Liberal in 1880. Became a peer in 1894. First Lord of the Admiralty 1905-8

Walsh, Stephen (1859-1929)
Miner. Labour MP for Ince 1906-29

Ward, John (1866-1934)
Early member of the SDF. Founded the Navvies' Union in 1889. A member of the GFTU executive. Lib-Lab MP for Stoke 1906-29

Wardle, George (1865-1947)
Member of the Amalgamated Society of Railway Servants. Editor of the *Railway Review* 1898-1919. Labour MP for Stockport 1906-20

Warwick, Lady Frances (1861-1938)
Member of SDF. Organiser of many social projects and provider of considerable funds for the SDF

Webb, Beatrice (1858-1943)
Socialist writer and historian. Member of the Fabian Society executive. Served on the poor law commission 1905-9 and was largely responsible for the minority report

Webb, Sidney (1859-1947)
Socialist, historian, and writer. Member of the Fabian Society executive. Member of the London County Coun-

cil (Progressive) 1892-1910

Wilkie, Alexander
(1850-1928)
General Secretary of the Ship Constructive and Shipwrights' Association 1882-1928. Member of the TUC Parliamentary Committee 1890-91, 1895-1903, 1904-9. Member of the Labour Party executive 1900-1904. Labour MP for Dundee 1906-22

Wilson, Joseph
Havelock
(1859-1929)
Founder of the seamen's union. Lib-Lab MP for Middlesbrough 1892-1900, 1906-10

Wilson, William
Tyson
(1855-1921)
Member of the Amalgamated Society of Carpenters and Joiners. Labour MP for Westhoughton 1906-21

Woods, Sam
(1846-1915)
Vice-President of the Miners' Federation of Great Britain 1889-1909. Secretary of the TUC 1894-1904. MP for Ince 1892-5, for Walthamstow 1897-1900

Bibliography

PART 1 PRIMARY SOURCES

PRIVATE PAPERS

H. Arnold-Forster	BM
H. H. Asquith	BL
A. J. Balfour	BM
G. Balfour	PRO
W. H. Beveridge	BLPES
A. Birrell	Liverpool University Library
R. Blatchford	Manchester Central Public Library
A. Bonar Law	BkL
A. J. Braithwaite	BLPES
H. Broadhurst	BLPES
H. Bryan	BLPES
J. Bryce	BL
J. Burns	BM
S. Buxton	C/o Mrs J. Clay, Newtimber Lodge, Hassocks, Sussex
H. Campbell-Bannerman	BM
A. Chamberlain	Birmingham University Library
J. Chamberlain	Birmingham University Library
Viscount Chilston	Kent County Archives Office
C. Dilke	BM
Master of Elibank	NLS
D. Lloyd George	BkL
E. Grey	PRO
R. B. Haldane	NLS
E. Hamilton	BM
G. Lansbury	BLPES

Lord Lansdowne	PRO
Viscount W. Long	Wiltshire County Record Office
J. R. MacDonald	BLPES
A. Mattison	Brotherton Library, University of Leeds
Lord Passfield	BLPES
Lord Ripon	BM
W. Runciman	Newcastle University Library
H. Samuel	House of Lords Record Office
H. J. Wilson	Sheffield Central Library

MANUSCRIPT AND PRINTED MINUTES ETC

Fabian Society, minutes and correspondence	NCL
ILP, Bristol branch minutes	BLPES
City of London branch minutes	BLPES
Metropolitan District Council minutes	BLPES
National Administrative Council minutes	BLPES
Reports and circulars from head office	BLPES
Sheffield branch minutes	Sheffield Central Library
Southwark branch minutes	BLPES
Watford branch minutes and correspondence	BLPES
West Ham branch minutes	BLPES
Joint Board, Minutes	Usually bound with the GFTU reports
LRC, Letter Files	Transport House Library
The infancy of the Labour Party	BLPES
SDF, Hackney branch minutes	Marx Memorial Library
TUC, PC minutes	Congress House
Woolwich Labour Representation Association, Minutes	Woolwich Labour Party
Woolwich Trades and Labour Council, Minutes	Woolwich Labour Party

COLLECTIONS OF DOCUMENTS, NEWSCUTTINGS, ETC

British Socialist Party collection	BLPES
Cooke collection	BLPES

Election addresses   NLC
Unemployment collection   BLPES

POLITICAL REPORTS

BSP, *Annual Report*
Fabian Society, *Annual Report*
ILP, *Annual Report*
    Report of a conference on destitution and unemploy-
       ment, 1910
Labour Party, *Annual Report*
        Quarterly Report
        Report of a special conference on unemploy-
         ment and the incidence of taxation, 1909
          The Labour Party and unemployment, 1908
National Liberal Federation, *Annual Report*
National Union of Conservative Associations, *Annual Report*
SDF, *Annual Report*

UNION REPORTS AND JOURNALS

Amalgamated Society of Carpenters	*Annual Report*
and Joiners	*Monthly Report*
Amalgamated Society of Engineers	*Annual Report*
	Monthly Report
Amalgamated Society of Operative	*Annual Report*
Cotton Spinners	*Quarterly Report*
Amalgamated Society of Railway	
Servants	*Annual Report*
Amalgamated Toolmakers Society	*Annual Report*
	Monthly Report
Associated Ironmoulders of Scotland	*Monthly Report*
Associated Shipwrights Society	*Annual Report*
	Quarterly Report
Dock, Wharf, Riverside and General	*Annual Report*
Workers Union	*Dockers Record*
Electrical Trade Union	*Eltradion*
Friendly Society of Ironfounders	*Annual Report*
	Monthly Report

General Federation of Trade Unions   *Proceedings and Reports*

General Union of Operative Carpenters *Half Yearly Report*
and Joiners

London Society of Compositors   *Annual Report*

London Trades Council   *Annual Report*

Miners Federation of Great Britain   *Annual Report*

National Amalgamated Furniture   *Annual Report*
Trade Union

National Amalgamated Union of   *Annual Report*
Labour   *Quarterly Report*

National Society of Brassworkers   *Annual Report*

National Union of Boot and Shoe   *Annual Report*
Operatives   *Monthly Report*

National Union of Carpenters and   *Annual Report*
Joiners

National Union of Dock Labourers   *Annual Report*

National Union of Gas Workers and   *Annual Report*
General Labourers   *Quarterly balance sheet*

Operative Bricklayers Society   *Annual Report*
                                                            Trades Circular and General Reporter

Postmen's Federation   *Annual Report*
                                                            Postmen's Gazette

Railway Clerks' Association   *Railway Clerk*

Society of Lithographic Printers   *Annual Report*

Trades Union Congress   *Annual Report*
                                                            Quarterly Circular

Typographical Association   *Half Yearly Report*
                                                            Typographical Circular

United Society of Boilermakers   *Annual Report*
                                                            Monthly Report

OFFICIAL PAPERS AND REPORTS
Board of Trade, *Annual Report*
     Labour Gazette
     Reports on unemployment and the state of
       trade
British Parliamentary Papers
Cabinet papers
Hansard
Local Government Board, *Annual Report*

NEWSPAPERS

1 Labour and socialist	2 National
British Socialist	*Daily Express*
Clarion	*Daily Graphic*
Clarion Scout	*Daily Mail*
Fabian News	*Daily News*
ILP News	*Daily Telegraph*
ILP Platform	*Morning Post*
Justice	*Observer*
Labour Leader	*Standard*
Railway Review	*The Times*
Reynold's Newspaper	*Westminster Gazette*
SDP News	
Socialist Record	
Trades and Labour Gazette	

CONTEMPORARY PERIODICALS

Charity Organisation Review	*Labour Record and Review*
Christian Commonwealth	*Liberal Magazine*
Contemporary Review	*National Review*
Cornhill Magazine	*National Union Gleanings*
Economic Journal	*New Age*
Economic Review	*Nineteenth Century*
English Review	*North American Review*
Independent Review	*Political Science Quarterly*

Quarterly Review   *Spectator*
Review of Reviews   *Toynbee Record*
Social Democrat   *Westminster Review*
Socialist Review

MISCELLANEOUS

Bristol Right to Work Committee, *Annual Report*
Charity Organisation Society, *Annual Report*
Conférence Internationale du chomâge, *Rapports,* 1910
National Free Labour Association, *Annual Report* (1909 only)
National Right to Work Council, *Report of a conference on
                                destitution and unemploy-
                                ment,* 1908

PART 2   SECONDARY   SOURCES

THIS LIST IS selective, comprising only those works which the
author found most useful in preparing this book.

CONTEMPORARY BOOKS AND PAMPHLETS

Alden, Percy. *The unemployed : a national question* (1905)
Barnes, George. *The unemployed problem* (1908)
Beveridge, William. *Unemployment : a problem of industry*
    (1909)
Burns, John. *Labour and drink* (1904)
                The unemployed (1893)
Churchill, Winston. *Liberalism and the social problem* (2nd
    ed, 1909)
Dearle, Norman. *Problems of unemployment in the London
    building trades* (1908)
Duffy, T. Gavan. *Mr Lloyd George's insurance scheme* (1911)
Fabian Society. *The National Insurance Bill* (1911)
Hardie, James Keir. *John Bull and his unemployed* (1905)
                The unemployed problem (1904)

Henderson, Arthur, and Barnes, George. *Unemployment in Germany* (1907)

Hobson, John. *The crisis of Liberalism* (1909)

Howell, George. *Trade unionism old and new* (1891)

Jackson, Cyril. *Unemployment and the trade unions* (1910)

Lansbury, George. *Unemployment—the next step* (1907)

London, Jack. *The people of the abyss* (1903)

LRC. *How the workers of the world began winter* (1905)
Protection perhaps, but what kind (1905)

MacDonald, James Ramsay. *The new Unemployed Bill of the Labour Party* (1907)

Mann, Tom. *The eight hours movement* (1891)
The programme of the ILP and the unemployed (1895)
and Tillett, Ben. *The new trades unionism* (1890)

Masterman, Charles. *From the abyss* (1902)
The condition of England (1909)

Money, Leo. *Insurance against unemployment* (1912)
Work for all (1909)

National Committee for the prevention of Destitution. *How to provide for the unemployed* (1911)
The prevention of unemployment (1911)

Rowntree, Benjamin, and Lasker, Bruno. *Unemployment : a social study* (1911)

Schloss, David. *Insurance against unemployment* (1909)

Smart, Harold. *The right to work* (1906)

Snowden, Philip. *The national insurance schemes explained* (1911)

Summerbell, Tom. *The unemployed and the land* (1908)

Taylor, Fanny. *A bibliography of unemployment and the unemployed* (1909)

Warwick, Countess of. *Unemployment* (1906)

BIOGRAPHY, AUTOBIOGRAPHY AND REMINISCENCE

Aldred, Guy. *No traitor's gait* (Glasgow, 1955)

Asquith, Herbert. *Fifty years of parliament* (two vols, 1926)
            Memories and reflections (two vols, 1928)

Barnes, George. *From workshop to war cabinet* (1924)

Bell, Tom. *Pioneering days* (1941)

Beveridge, William. *Power and influence : an autobiography* (1953)

Brockway, Fenner. *Socialism over sixty years* (1946)

Churchill, Randolph. *Winston S. Churchill. Vol II. Young statesman, 1901-1914* (1966)

Clynes, John. *Memoirs* (two vols, 1937)

George, Richard Lloyd. *Lloyd George* (1960)

George, William. *My brother and I* (1958)

Gould, Frederick. *Hyndman, prophet of socialism, 1842-1921* (1928)

Hamilton, Mary. *Arthur Henderson. A biography* (1938)

Haw, George. *The life story of Will Crooks MP* (1917)

Hyndman, Henry. *Further reminiscences* (1912)
            The record of an adventurous life (1911)

Jackson, Thomas. *Solo trumpet* (1953)

Kent, William. *John Burns : labour's lost leader* (1950)

Lansbury, George. *My life* (1928)

McKenna, Stephen. *Reginald McKenna, 1863-1943* (1948)

Mann, Tom. *Memoirs* (1923)

Masterman, Lucy. *C. F. G. Masterman* (1939)

Montefiore, Dora. *From a Victorian to a modern* (1927)

Owen, Frank. *Tempestuous journey* (1954)

Redfern, Percy. *Journey to understanding* (1946)

Riddell, Lord. *More pages from my diary, 1908-1914* (1934)

Samuel, Herbert. *Memoirs* (1945)

Sanders, William. *Early socialist days* (1927)

Snowden, Philip. *An autobiography* (two vols, 1934)

Spender, John. *The life of the Rt Hon Sir Henry Campbell-Bannerman* (two vols, 1923) and Asquith, Cyril. *The life of Herbert Henry Asquith* (two vols, 1932)

Stewart, William. *J. Keir Hardie. A biography* (1921)

Tallents, Stephen. *Man and boy* (1943)

Thomson, Malcolm. *Lloyd George. The official biography* (1945)

Thorne, Will. *My life's battles* (1925)

Tillett, Ben. *Memories and reflections* (1931)

Tsuzuki, Chushichi. *H. M. Hyndman and British socialism* (Oxford, 1961)

Webb, Beatrice. *My apprenticeship* (1950)
Our partnership (1948)

WORKS ON LABOUR HISTORY

Bealey, Frank, and Pelling, Henry. *Labour and politics, 1900-1906* (1958)

Beer, Max. *History of British socialism* (two vols, 1929)

Brand, Carl. *The British Labour Party* (Stamford, 1964)

Clayton, Joseph. *Rise and decline of socialism, 1884-1924* (1926)

Clegg, Hugh, Fox, Alan, and Thompson, Arthur. *History of British trade unionism since 1889* (Oxford, 1964)

Cole, George D. H. *British working class politics, 1832-1914* (1941)

Cole, Margaret. *The story of Fabian socialism* (1961)

Dowse, Robert. *Left in the centre. The ILP 1883-1940* (1966)

Gregory, Roy. *The miners and British politics, 1906-1914* (1968)

Kendall, Walter. *The revolutionary movement in Britain, 1900-1921* (1969)

Lovell, John. *Stevedores and dockers : a study of trade unionism in the Port of London* (1969)

McBriar, Alan. *Fabian socialism and English politics, 1884-1914* (1962)

Miliband, Ralph. *Parliamentary socialism* (1961)

Pease, Edward. *The history of the Fabian Society* (2nd ed,
      1925)
Pelling, Henry. *A history of British trade unionism* (1963)
                *Popular politics and society in late Victorian
                      Britain* (1968)
                Short history of the Labour Party (1961)
                The origins of the Labour Party (1953)
Poirier, Philip. *The advent of the Labour Party* (1958)
Roberts, Benjamin. *The Trades Union Congress, 1868-1921*
      (1958)
Tate, George. *The London Trades Council, 1860-1950* (1950)
Thompson, Paul. *Socialists, Liberals, and Labour* (1967)
Webb, Sidney and Beatrice. *History of trade unionism* (1920)

GENERAL BACKGROUND WORKS
Adams, William. *Edwardian heritage, 1901-1906* (1949)
Bruce, Maurice. *The coming of the welfare state* (1961)
Bunbury, Henry (ed). *Lloyd George's ambulance wagon*
      (1957)
Gilbert, Bentley. *The evolution of national insurance in Great
      Britain* (1966)
Halévy, Elie. *The rule of democracy* (1934)
Mowatt, Charles. *The Charity Organisation Society* (1961)
Nowell-Smith, Simon (ed). *Edwardian England, 1900-1914*
      (1964)
Pelling, Henry. *Social geography of British elections, 1885-
      1910* (1967)
Phelps Brown, Ernest. *The growth of British industrial
      relations* (1959)
Sayers, Richard. *A history of economic change in England,
      1880-1939* (1967)
Williams, Gertrude. *The state and the standard of living*
      (1936)

ARTICLES AND THESES

Blewett, Neal. *The British general elections of 1910* (Oxford
D Phil thesis, 1967)

Brown, John. *Ideas concerning social policy and their inflence
on legislation in Britain, 1902-1911* (London PhD thesis,
1964)

Brown, Kenneth. *Labour and unemployment, 1900-1914*
(Kent PhD thesis, 1969)

Marwick, Arthur. 'The Labour Party and the welfare state in
Britain, 1900-1948', *American Historical Review*, 73 (Dec
1967), 380-403

Russell, Anthony. *The general election of 1906* (Oxford
D Phil thesis, 1962)

Tsuzuki, Chushichi. 'The impossibilist revolt in Britain', *International Review of Social History*, 1 (1956), 377-97

Acknowledgements

I WISH TO thank the following individuals and institutions for permission to quote from papers in their keeping: the Trustees of the British Museum for the papers of Balfour, Burns, Campbell-Bannerman, Herbert Gladstone and Lord Ripon; the Bodleian Library, Oxford, and Mr Mark Bonham Carter for the Asquith papers; the British Library of Political and Economic Science for the Lansbury, Beveridge and Herbert Bryan archives; the Passfield Trustees for the Passfield Collection; the Right Hon the Viscount Chilston and Kent County Council for the Akers-Douglas papers; Newcastle University for the papers of Walter Runciman; the Trustees of the National Library of Scotland for the Elibank papers; Beaverbrook Newspapers Ltd for the Lloyd George papers; the Fabian Society for their records held at Nuffield College; and Mrs J. Clay for permission to consult the papers of her grandfather, Sidney Buxton.

Librarians, archivists and trade union officers too numerous to list individually all gave generously of their time and knowledge, for which I am very grateful. My colleague in the Department of Economic and Social History at Queen's, Max Goldstrom, kindly read the draft manuscript and offered several helpful criticisms. Above all, my thanks are due to Professor F. S. L. Lyons of the University of Kent who will recognise in this book a much amended version of the doctoral thesis which he supervised between 1966 and 1969.

Kenneth D. Brown

Queen's University, Belfast

Index